EXPLOITING
POKER TELLS

EXPLOITING POKER TELLS

ZACHARY ELWOOD

Via Regia, LLC
viaregiapublishing.com

Exploiting Poker Tells

For information, contact:
www.ViaRegiaPublishing.com
info@viaregiapublishing.com

ISBN: 978-0-9840333-5-5

"Most of the money you'll win at poker comes not from the brilliance of your own play, but from the ineptitude of your opponents."

- Lou Krieger, poker player and author

Contents

Acknowledgements

Many thanks to these people for helping me with the book: **Cyrus Nemani** for feedback; **Ed Walters** for feedback; **Chris Saroka** for feedback; **Mike Lynch** for feedback, **Molly Elwood** for proofreading; **Alina Baloi** for front cover artwork; **John Paul Dull** for cover design; and **Allison Cook** for interior layout.

And thanks to everyone who helped out by providing hand histories, or giving input on the book title, cover, quiz, and content.

Introduction

This book is the third in a trilogy that includes my first two books *Reading Poker Tells* and *Verbal Poker Tells*.

Exploiting Poker Tells is meant to stand on its own; it's not necessary for you to have read my first two books to understand and enjoy this one. However, it will help to have read them, because those books go into more detail on some of the general concepts and tells mentioned in passing in this book. But again, it's not necessary.

This book will also be my last poker-related book, with the main reason being: I don't think there will be too much left to say on the subject after this, at least not enough to justify an entire book. It's my hope that this trilogy will be widely regarded as the best books on the subject for a long time. When I do have some new and interesting thoughts, I'll create a new video for my video series (readingpoker-tells.video), or update my existing books.

The reason I decided to write this book is that I believe my understanding of physical tells has improved over the last few years. There are a few reasons for this:

- I was a paid consultant for two World Series of Poker Main Event 'November Niners' (i.e., players who made the final table). I was hired by Amir Lehavot in 2013, who got 3rd place, and by Max Steinberg in 2015, who got 4th. My work involved studying footage of the final table players and looking for behavioral patterns. I've also done some private consultation for some high-stakes cash game players and tournament players, which involved some video analysis and webinar presentations. This work has forced me to think more about high-level, serious players and their behavior and thought processes, which helped me to understand poker behavior better in general.

- I wrote a monthly column for Bluff Magazine (now out of business) for about a year and a half, starting in 2013 and ending in late 2014. For some of my articles, I interviewed professional players about their thoughts on poker tells. This gave me additional insight on how experienced players thought about the subject. I've included some of these interviews in this book.

- In 2015, I started work on my poker tells video series (available at ReadingPokerTells.video). The series uses real poker footage from both cash games and tournaments. Forcing myself to study this game footage in-depth and find patterns gave me additional insight into how common and reliable certain behaviors were.

- My main goal with this book is to give practical advice on how to use tells. I've had many readers tell me they enjoyed my books and videos, but that they struggled to make use of the information in practice, at the table. With this book, I wanted to talk more about how to best make use of the things you notice. Not just about what things mean, but *what to do about it when you see them.*

The major questions this book is meant to focus on are:

What are the factors involved in making a good read? What factors should cause us to use behavior in a decision versus relying on fundamental strategy?

These are difficult questions.

They're difficult because poker strategy itself is so complex. It's hard enough to confidently say what an optimal strategy is, even in the absence of tells. No-limit poker is a more complex game than chess and it's far from being solved in a game-theory-optimal (GTO) way. Even for many situations that would seem quite simple on the surface, you will find expert-level players debating the optimal strategy.

When you throw opponent behavior into the mix—which is subjective and debatable itself—and you begin to think about optimal ways to incorporate that behavior into your strategy, things are understandably very complex and hard to talk about in clear ways.

By the way, this is a good spot to point out that I am not an expert-level poker strategist. I'm a decent player, sure, but there are many, many players more skilled than me at fundamental poker strategy. I have admittedly not focused on that part of my game. I fully recognize my own strategic weaknesses and I want to give that disclaimer up-front.

What this means is: *I don't pretend that my thoughts in this book are the only or best way to make use of behavioral information.* Even assuming most of my general ideas about poker behavior are correct, that doesn't mean that I know the optimal way to make use of that information in every situation. The most I can do is to give you my ideas and why I think they make sense.

That being said, no one else that I know of has written as much about the practical side of using tells as I have. Most poker tell content out there talks about behavior in a simplistic "this means that" way, and my goal has always been to delve into details as much as possible.

I believe my first book made good progress in talking about the importance of situational factors: I separated poker tells into categories of Waiting-For-Action, During-Action, and Post-Bet, and for the first time, there was a general framework for thinking about tells. That's what many people have said they liked the most about that book; that it was not just a compilation of tells, but that it gave a mental structure for interpreting tells.

With *Exploiting Poker Tells*, I hope to take that conversation to the next level, and talk about the specific factors that can be present during a hand and how they can affect your decision-making process.

I encourage you to think for yourself and to form your own opinions. If you're an experienced player and you disagree with me on something, I'd appreciate hearing your thoughts.

Organization

This book is broken up into three main sections:

- Pre-flop tells
- Flop and turn tells
- River tells

These sections will feature behavior that mainly occurred in the given round or rounds of play. Obviously there can be a lot of situational overlap between streets, so this is an approximate grouping. The river is separated from the flop and turn because it's unique in being both a big-bet spot and also a final action-ending situation where no draws are possible.

I structured the book by round of play to emphasize that poker behavior can be affected by round-based factors like 1) the size of the pot, 2) the amount of thinking and potential play left in the hand, and 3) how well-defined a player's hand is, which is related to how many cards are left to come.

I've included the most practically useful behaviors, while purposefully leaving out ideas that were too speculative, ambiguous, or hard to make practical use of.

Even though I've organized the book into rounds specific to Hold'em and Omaha, the information should apply to all poker games.

There is a quiz at the end of the book, and a link to an online version of the quiz.

Notes about hands used, the players, and the games

All of the hands in this book are real hands. The majority of these hands happened exactly as I've described (or as close to exact as I can deduce from my notes). For some hands, I've changed some details to make them more clear or more educational. Examples of things I've changed include:

- Changing an observed hand to first-person point-of view to make it more interactive and educational

- Changing bet sizes or boards to better illustrate a concept

- Leaving out things that happened in the hand that I thought were distracting or irrelevant

Many of the hand histories come from hands I played or observed in a rake-free game in Portland, Oregon. You might notice that pot sizes don't have rake subtracted from them, and that is why. To keep it consistent, and to have even numbers for pot size, I've used the same approach even for hands from raked games. The few dollars difference in pot size in those hands shouldn't matter for our purposes.

This book gives examples from both cash games and tournaments, and most of the tells will apply to both game types. Worth noting, though: there will be more practically useful behavior in cash games, because people are generally more relaxed and less on-guard in cash games.

For the hand histories, I avoided referencing the stack sizes for every hand, as I felt that would make the hands harder to read and needlessly complex. If stack size is not mentioned, it's because I thought the stack size wasn't that relevant to the discussion. For cash game hand histories without stack sizes, you can assume an average stack of around 100 BBs.

I sometimes get the question: "Why don't you talk about bet-sizing tells?" The main reason is that I don't consider bet-sizing patterns to be poker tells. To me, a *tell* involves physical or verbal behavior. Interpreting bet-sizing is a fundamental part of poker, and I consider it more on the strategy-side of things. In the same way, I don't think of someone's looseness or tightness as a tell, even though that can give you a lot of information about a player's hand. I do talk about bet-sizing patterns a few times in this book, but it's far from the focus.

Some general concepts

You'll notice some general ideas that come up frequently in the hand histories in this book. Here are these general ideas:

- Most reliable tells can be separated into categories of *Non-Aggressor* (i.e., checkers, callers, and players waiting for an opponent to act) and *Associated With A Significant Bet*. This is because making a significant bet involves different motivations and feelings than being the non-aggressor in the hand, and this leads to differences in how tells show up. (These categories correlate to categories in my first book. *Non-Aggressor* is similar to the *Waiting-For-Action* category in my first book, and *Associated With A Significant Bet* is similar to the *Post-Bet* category. My thinking on these categories has evolved a bit and I've broadened the definitions.)

- Early in a hand, when the pot is small, players with strong hands, whether aggressors or non-aggressors, are both more mentally focused and stoic and also, with their strongest hands, don't like to draw attention to themselves. This accounts for why, early in a hand, most unusual, ostentatious (attention-grabbing) behavior comes from players with weak and medium-strength hands. *Most reliable weak-hand tells will be from players who are non-aggressors and/or waiting-to-act.*

- When a hand is almost over, players making large bets with strong hands are more relaxed and more willing to do and say unusual things, while bluffers are more likely to be physically stoic and quiet. For players making big bets, unusual or ostentatious behavior will make strong hands more likely. (Note how this is the opposite of unusual and ostentatious behavior that happens early in a hand.) *Most reliable strong-hand tells will be from players who've made a large bet.*

- Most during-hand talking comes from a) non-aggressors who have weak hands and who are speaking defensively and b) players who've made big bets with strong hands and are speaking due to being relaxed.

- Most behavior, whether physical or verbal, falls into what I call the "first level" of deception. In other words, most behavior will adhere to the well-known 'strong-behavior-means-weak-hand' and 'weak-behavior-means-strong-hand' pattern that Mike Caro popularized in his classic *Book of Poker Tells*.

- Players who have played a lot of poker, whether they're actually good or bad players, are more capable of performing false tells or reverse tells; in other words, doing the opposite of the commonly understood behaviors in a tricky "second-level" way. In practice, though, purposeful reverse tells are fairly rare because most experienced players are focused on staying stoic and unreadable, and don't want to get into complex and confusing mental "leveling" wars with opponents.

- Most of the time, you'll want to study an opponent a bit and have a sense of their past behavior before acting on a tell. You'll want to *correlate* a player's behavior with specific hand strengths in specific situations, as much as you're able. "Cold reads," with no knowledge of a player's past behavior, should generally be avoided. Sometimes it's fine to make a cold read if you're confident your opponent is a recreational player and the pattern is a common, reliable one.

- When considering basing a decision on opponent behavior: the more money is at risk, the more evidence you would want that the behavior is actually a reliable indicator of a certain hand strength. (But a poker tell doesn't have to be super-reliable to be actionable. Even a tell that is only slightly correlated to a certain hand strength can be useful, assuming you're using it in spots where you're unsure of what to do from a strategic perspective.)

- A tell can be both *highly reliable* and *infrequent*. For example, a player might have a 100% reliable tell that indicates a strong hand when he bets the river, but that tell might only show up 5% of the time he value-bets on the river. In other words, the tell will always indicate a strong hand, but he won't often display that tell, which means there's not much meaning there when the behavior isn't present. In other words: *the absence of a poker tell is not necessarily a tell.*

- Building on the point above: *the more frequent a tell is, the more meaning its absence contains.* Let's say a player has a 100% reliable tell that indicates a strong-hand river bet, and it shows up 80% of the time when he value-bets the river. In that case, the lack of that behavior is also now a very reliable tell of a weak hand. *For most tells, though, the frequency will be fairly low, meaning the opposite of that behavior will not be nearly as meaningful.*

Here is a table summarizing the underlying ideas behind many of the behavioral patterns in this book:

Situation ↓	Hand strength		
	Strong hands	Medium-strength hands	Weak hands
Non-aggressors at any point in hand	Non-aggressors with strong hands generally avoid drawing attention to themselves and are more mentally focused and stoic. (But so are most players.)	Behavior varies a lot.	Non-aggressors with weak hands are more prone to exhibiting unusual and ostentatious behavior, often in a defensive way.
Aggressors: Early-in-hand or small-bets	Bettors with strong hands, when pot is small, are generally more mentally focused and avoid drawing attention to themselves.	Behavior varies a lot.	Players with weak hands, when pot is small, are more capable of unusual and ostentatious behaviors, mainly due to being less mentally focused.
Aggressors: Large bets or shoves	Players making big bets with strong hands are capable of doing unusual or ostentatious things. Reasons: a) they are relaxed, b) there is nothing left to think about, and c) the pot is a decent size so there is less fear of scaring opponents away.	Medium-strength shoves are rare post-flop. Pre-flop shoves fall in this category and there will be a good amount of variety.	Players making big bluffs are reserved and restrained in their behavior. (But so are most players making big bets.)

This chart is online at www.readingpokertells.com/chart, and I may update it and add to it in future. So feel free to check that URL to see if my thoughts on these general patterns have changed.

Keep these general ideas in mind as you read this book, and check them out again once you're done reading.

The overall importance of tells

An opponent's behavior should only infrequently sway your decision. For the most part, your decisions should be based on fundamental strategy.

When I play a typical day-long session of poker, whether it's a cash game or tournament, an opponent's behavior might influence a decision of mine maybe three to five times. I might *notice* many more poker tells, but the actual spots where I end up basing a decision on one are fairly infrequent. And that's mainly a function of how few hands you will typically be playing at an average, full table.

When an opponent's behavior does influence me, much of the time it will just be a small pre-flop clue in a situation that could go one of several ways to begin with. (For example, someone's pre-flop behavior might influence me to make a light three-bet instead of a fold or a call.) Some days, especially at more serious higher-stakes games, I can go all day and not act on a read. Other days, there might be a player in the game whose tells are very reliable, which will cause me to base more decisions on tells.

Some inexperienced poker players can have an inflated, unrealistic sense of what is possible with tells. So I want to reiterate: *tells are a minor part of playing strong live poker.*

Wrong reads are inevitable

It's important to understand: *when you decide to incorporate poker tells into your game, your reads will sometimes be wrong.*

This is completely expected and inevitable. For all exploitative strategies (i.e., strategies aimed at exploiting opponent flaws), your decision will sometimes be wrong in a specific hand.

To give a strategic, non-tell-related comparison: when an opponent has been three-betting pre-flop every single hand, and you make an exploitative decision to four-bet him light, he will sometimes have pocket aces. *This doesn't mean your exploitative decision was wrong.* You made your decision because you thought it would be profitable in the long run. You hopefully didn't expect that it would be correct *every* time you did it.

In the same way, acting on opponent behavior is a numbers game. If you have a read that is slightly reliable, or even very reliable, it will sometimes be "wrong" in the context of a single hand. This doesn't necessarily mean that it was a bad read.

I wanted to point this out because I think some people, when they make a read and it turns out to be wrong, get frustrated with trying to use poker tells. This is understandable, because it *is* frustrating to make a move or a fold based on a read, only to discover you were completely off-base. You're using a more speculative source of information, so it is understandable that it stings more when you're wrong. "If I'd only played the hand the *normal* way," you might think, "that wouldn't have happened."

But you should remember that, if you're reading opponents well in general, you will be right more often than you are wrong and your reads will improve your results. It's just usually much easier to remember the times you were wrong than the times you were right.

Okay, let's get to the hands.

Pre-Flop Tells

Before the flop, hand strength is usually undefined. In Hold'em, pocket Aces and Kings are the only hands most players are genuinely glad to get a lot of action with pre-flop. With all other hands, including Ace-King and pocket Queens, most players in most situations will be fairly ambivalent until they see the flop. This means that getting reliable reads pre-flop will usually be difficult. Sometimes, though, there are small behavioral clues that can influence you to take a more cautious or aggressive approach.

Players with premium hands (~TT+, AK, AQ) are generally more focused and stoic. One reason is that they have more to actually think about. Another factor is that players with the strongest hands (mainly KK and AA) don't like to draw attention to themselves or scare away action. The practical upshot of these tendencies is that ostentatious, attention-grabbing behavior pre-flop will tend to weaken a player's range. This is true for both bettors and non-aggressors.

Hand #1: Various pre-flop weak-hand behaviors
$2-5 NLHE cash game

I'm in the hijack position (two seats before the dealer button) with T♠ 7♠. Everyone folds to me.

Behind me, both the cutoff (the seat before the button) and the button have already looked at their cards. I see the cutoff shuffling his cards, which for him, as it does for many players, means he's probably going to be folding.

The button is a fairly predictable player, on the tighter side. After looking at his cards, he puts a chip on his cards with a loud slap, and he starts to riffle his chips.

If the button had a premium hand (approximately JJ+, AK), he'd likely be more mentally focused and more stoic. He'd be thinking ahead about what to do and this would make him more gentle in his movements. Also, with his strongest hands (AA and KK), it's likely he wouldn't want to place a chip loudly on his cards because:

- It draws attention to him

- It announces his interest in playing

And players with AA and KK don't like to draw attention to themselves before it's their turn to act.

Now, obviously this player *will* sometimes have a strong hand. This ostentatious behavior is just a general indicator making weak hands more likely. And even if this read were 100% reliable as a weaker range, some strong hands like TT and AQ could still easily be in his range. But the point is: *his unusual, ostentatious behavior before action gets to him makes strong hands less likely than they otherwise would be.*

Besides the behavior of the two players behind me, the players in the blinds are very tight and predictable. I know they will usually be folding. If they do call, they will often be playing very tight and predictably post-flop.

All of these factors encourage me to raise. I make it $15.

There are several factors here, and they all line up favorably to encourage me to take a more aggressive line. If it were just the behavior of the players behind me, that info wouldn't be enough to overcome the weakness of my hand or the number of players still to act. But when you add in the tighter playing styles of the blinds and the button, such a play starts to make more sense.

I think it's possible that you could raise profitably here with any two cards. In any case, it's a good spot for raising some decent hands that would otherwise be folds without the extra information.

These kinds of clues are why it's important to pay attention to the players behind you. Spotting small signs of weakness from players behind you can influence you to take a more aggressive approach.

After I raise, the cutoff folds and the button thinks for a few seconds, then three-bets to $60. The blinds fold. The button has about $600 and I have him covered.

I believe the button's behavior makes AA and KK significantly less likely than usual. AK and JJ make up his most probable range. QQ is possible but less likely than normal due to his ostentatious behavior. Mathematically, he's most likely to have AK. Knowing what I know of his playing style, I know he will often be folding most of his range, including AK, to a four-bet. I make it $210 and he folds after a few seconds.

Hand #2: Weak-hand behavior from limpers
$1-2 NLHE cash game

I'm in the big blind with Q♥ 7♣. There are four limps in early position. Three of these players, including the UTG player, put their chips in very ostentatiously, slamming or tossing them in with a lot of force. Two of the players double-check their cards after limping. One player stares at his cards for a few seconds.

These ostentatious behaviors make weak hands more likely. Players limping strong hands will usually do so calmly and stoically, so the ostentatious placement of chips makes strong hands less likely.

The double-checking of hole cards and the staring at hole cards are similar behavior. Players with strong hands don't like to draw attention to their cards. Players with strong hands often have an instinct to "hide their treasure" and will usually put those cards down quickly. While it's common for players to double-check their hole cards between rounds (e.g., right before the flop comes out), these kinds of double-checking and staring behaviors during a round, from non-aggressors, will make weak hands more likely.

It's fairly common in low-limit games for players to limp in UTG or UTG+1 with AA or KK, hoping for a raise so that they can reraise. This should cross your mind as a possibility when you see a tight player limping early. *When an early-position player limps in with AA or KK, they'll usually act inconspicuously. They'll put their chips in gently, they'll act calmly, they'll look distracted, they'll not want to draw attention to themselves.* Little ostentatious behaviors can encourage you to take a more aggressive line, if other factors also align.

Back to the hand:

The small blind calls, making the pot $12. I raise to $28 and everyone folds.

If my hand were weaker, or if my in-position opponents were very "sticky" (calling a lot), I wouldn't do this. I do want something somewhat decent in case I'm called, which a good amount of the time I will be. At the same time, if I'm called I will often be taking the pot down post-flop, so it's arguable that this could be done with even weaker hands.

Hand #3: Weak-hand limping behavior, bet-sizing
$2-5 NLHE cash game

A player limps under-the-gun and slams his chip down in front of him. I know this player is capable of limping with AA and KK, so this ostentatious behavior makes it unlikely he has those hands this time.

A middle-position player, who's pretty loose but not very aggressive, makes it $20. From experience, I know this is a below-average raise for this player. If he were first-in, he'd usually make it $20 or more, so considering there's been one limper, this is small.

These kinds of lower-than-usual raises are a common bet-sizing pattern amongst low-stakes regulars: it will often indicate medium-strength hands with potential like AT, JTs, low pairs, hands like that. These smaller raises reflect the player's ambivalence about the hand (e.g., "I know I should raise with this hand but I'm not that excited about it") or, with suited connectors and small pairs, they don't actually mind a lot of callers and so the raise serves as a pot-builder in case they hit their hand post-flop. With strong hands, though, these players want to protect their hands more and prevent a big multi-way pot. (I'm not defending this thought process; I'm merely explaining why these bet-sizing patterns are so common.)

I have A♣ 8♣ and make it $60. Both players fold. The first raiser shows me A♠ J♥.

If it wasn't for the UTG player's ostentatious behavior, I would have been concerned that he might be limping with AA/KK and I wouldn't have thought the spot was good enough for a three-bet.

Hand #4: Weak-hand behavior from players behind

$300 buy-in NLHE tournament

After ten hours of play, we're nearing the bubble of this tournament.

There are only six players at my table. The blinds are 1,000-2,000 with a 200 ante. I have only 11 BBs, and most of the table has similar stacks. I'm UTG+1 with Q♦ T♣. The players in the blinds are very tight.

UTG folds and I'm next to act. This would usually be a clear fold for me, with four players still to act. But as I pause for a few seconds (as I usually do in significant tournament spots), the players behind me look at their cards.

The player directly behind me goes to muck out of turn, pitching her cards forward, then pulling them back quickly when she realizes I haven't acted yet. She's a bad player and I'm confident this is an actual mistake and not some sort of angle-shoot; I'm confident she'll be folding.

The player behind her stares at her cards steadily for several seconds. This makes it unlikely she's looking at a premium hand. (More on that later.)

All these factors (including the blinds being very tight) contribute to making this a good spot to shove.

I shove and the two players behind me fold. The big blind calls with A♥ K♣.

Hand #5: Subdued behavior from player behind
$550 buy-in NLHE tournament

I've been playing for a few hours at the same tournament table. The table has been fairly tight overall.

Everyone folds around to me. I have K♣ 8♦ on the button. I have about 30 BBs and the blinds have me covered. There are no antes yet.

The small blind is an older gentleman who has played mostly pretty tight. I've been observing his pre-flop behavior for a while (because I make it a habit to study the two or three players behind me). His usual behavior is to look at his cards and watch as the action goes around the table. His body language is usually fairly loose and normal; his body and face have small, normal movements as he watches the action.

In this hand, though, as I pause before raising, I notice that this man is looking down at the table in front of him and is very still. Compared to his usual behavior, this is unusual.

K-8 in this spot is a clear raise from the button, especially against tighter opponents, but I decide to fold based on the small blind's suspiciously subdued behavior.

After I fold, the small blind raises and the big blind folds.

For pre-flop decisions that are a bit borderline to begin with, a tell can help sway your decision, even if you think it's only slightly reliable.

Hand #6: Subdued behavior from early limper
$2-5 NLHE cash game

A player with only $250 limps UTG.

From experience, I know this player likes to limp strong hands early, even AK and AQ, with the intention of raising or shoving, depending on how much action there is after his limp.

He puts his chip in very gently and starts to nonchalantly look at his phone. This player's inconspicuous behavior makes it more likely than average that he's limped with a strong hand.

I have T♣ T♦ on the button. Considering TT isn't that strong a hand, there aren't too many downsides to limping with TT and treating it like a smaller pair. Also, I'd hate to be raised off my hand if he's going to three-bet big with AK or AQ, which I think he's sometimes capable of doing. So I opt to just call.

This player ends up showing K♠ K♣.

Worth noting: the *lack* of ostentatious behavior is not very meaningful, while the *presence* of ostentatious behavior is quite meaningful. In other words: *the absence of a reliable weak-hand tell isn't necessarily a reliable strong-hand tell.* This is because being stoic and unreadable is the standard behavior in most spots for most players. So there's not as much information when they stick to that general script.

So this player's lack of ostentatious behavior doesn't make me confident he has a strong hand; it just makes it slightly more likely that he's got a strong hand. Whereas if he displayed some ostentatious behavior when limping, it'd make it significantly more likely that he had a weaker hand.

Part of my decision to take this line with TT is that it's not that strong. If I had JJ+ I would still be raising, just because his behavior is not reliable enough information to dissuade me from raising with a hand that strong. But considering my opponent's limp-shove-type habits combined with his behavior, it's enough to get me to just call with weaker hands I'd usually be raising with, like TT, 99, AK, and AQ.

Hand #7: Emphatic verbal call from limper
$550 buy-in NLHE tournament

It's early in a tournament, with the average stack being around 200 BBs. An older man, a tight player, limps UTG+1 and says, "Call" a bit emphatically.

Everyone else folds. I'm on the button with 9♣ 7♥. I raise.

Verbal behavior is similar to physical behavior. Ostentatious verbal behavior from limpers and waiting-to-act players will make strong hands less likely. Verbal calls and checks can also have a defensive aspect to them: players (sometimes unconsciously) make verbal announcements with weak hands to convey their confidence. *The more os-*

tentatious the verbal behavior seems, the more likely it becomes that the player is on the weaker side.

Even though it may seem to be a pretty minor piece of information, verbal calls and checks can be a good early-hand decision-maker when you're on the fence about something. In this specific hand, without this player's verbal call, I would probably have folded, as he struck me as a player who was capable of limping UTG with strong hands.

Also worth noting: *you should be more likely to act on these small clues the bigger your stack is.* Because it's far from 100% reliable, especially in a vacuum, I'm less likely to act on such clues the more significant the spot it is. For example, if I only had 10 BBs or so here, I'd be unlikely to rely on small clues like this, because the risk of the read being wrong is much greater. This is one reason these kinds of small pre-flop clues tend to be more useful in deeper spots (like in cash games), where you can maneuver more post-flop.

This player turned out to have A♦ 2♦.

Hand #8: Pre-flop call with verbal statement

$550 NLHE tournament

This is from the same tournament as the preceding hand history and happens just a few minutes later.

It's folded around to the blinds. I'm in the big blind with 9♦ 4♥. The small blind, an inexperienced player, calls and says, "I'll just call."

Again: *these small early-hand verbal clues will be associated with weakness.* If this player had decided to trap with a strong hand, it's unlikely he'd say anything. Also, "I'll just call" is a slight misdirection, implying "I could have raised with this hand, but I'll *only* call."

I would usually just check here but this player's statement influenced me to raise.

This player had K♠ 9♣.

This player's statement, implying that he could have raised, probably had some truth to it. He probably *did* consider raising. But the point is that he'd be unlikely to say that with a premium hand.

Hand #9: The phone call read
$2-5 NLHE cash game

There's a businessman who plays regularly in this game. He often takes phone calls at the table. His phone calls are more important to him than the game, so he'll sometimes get a phone call and just muck out of turn so that he can take the call.

In this hand, this player is in the small blind and his phone starts to ring at the start of the hand. Instead of answering it, he just waits inconspicuously, not moving or saying anything, as action goes around.

I notice this player's behavior and know he must have a very strong hand. He doesn't often even raise with AK, so I know he would be mucking AK and medium-sized pairs to answer his phone. Plus his quiet, still pose as he waits for action makes it even more likely that he's strong.

There are three limps. I have A♦ Q♠ in late position and fold it. Sure enough, the small blind raises to $50. He ends up showing A♠ A♣.

Not the kind of situation that comes up often, but it does demonstrate the importance of paying attention.

Hand #10: Leaks of interest and disinterest
$5-10 and $2-5 NLHE cash games

The player I'll be talking about was one of the strongest players in the $5-10 and $2-5 NLHE games that I was playing in at the time. He was aggressive and chose good spots for light three-bets and four-bets.

He also had a pretty big leak. He would regularly make it obvious when he was going to be folding pre-flop. When the action was several spots in front of him, he'd often hold his cards up and move them around loosely, as if ready to muck. When he had an interesting hand that he might want to call or raise with, he'd be more subdued and still.

Because of this oversight in his play, he was not nearly the threat that he would have otherwise been. When he sat in a seat one or two to my left, I would often get a sense of his level of interest in the hand.

What were the practical benefits of noticing these things?

For one, I would be less restrained in raising if I saw a good spot for a light raise or three-bet.

For example, let's say there were several limps and I was in late position, considering a light raise. With this player right behind me, I would also have to worry that he saw the same situation I did and that, if I raised, he might three-bet or four-bet me light. But if I saw him distractedly holding his cards up, not looking focused on the situation, I'd feel much safer raising.

Another example: Say there was a limp and a few calls and I had a borderline hand that I was tempted to call with. If I saw this player behind me acting in a calm, interested way, I'd be more likely to just fold. That's because if he's interested in the situation there's an above-average chance he'll be raising. And even if he ended up just calling and not raising, I would still have to contend with this strong player behind me post-flop.

Here's one example of a hand where this player's behavior came into play:

It's a $5-10 NLHE cash game. There's a Mississippi straddle: this is where the button puts out $20 and action starts on the small blind.

I'm UTG with K♠ Q♦ and start to muck, but I'd forgotten about the straddle. The dealer points out the action isn't on me yet and I retrieve my cards.

The small blind and the big blind, both loose-passive players, limp for the $20 straddle, and now action is on me. With the $60 in the pot, and the two weak players in the blinds, I'm tempted to raise. I also think if I raise now, after trying to muck prematurely, some players will be suspicious of the weirdness of this and suspect that I was angle-shooting with AA or KK. Even though I would never actually do such a thing, my opponents don't know that and I think I might get some folds I might otherwise not get.

But as I pause for a few seconds I see the player in question right behind me, just sitting calmly, his hands over his cards, waiting patiently. Considering his early position and apparent interest, this is a bad sign, so I opt to fold. He raises to $80.

Hand #11: Genuine lack of interest

$1,500 buy-in NLHE WSOP tournament

There are many serious, strong players in this $1,500 WSOP tournament. As described in the last hand, some players, despite being good, are still capable of letting their level of interest be known.

In this tournament, there's an experienced player who looks at his cards early and who will sometimes make it obvious when he's not interested in the hand.

When he has a hand that has potential (one he might call or raise with), he will remain focused on the action. For example, say he's on the button and looks down at AK or JTs or a low pair. *He's motivated to watch the action as it goes around and pay attention to what's going on.*

He will sometimes pay attention to the action when he holds non-strong hands, too, so his attention to the action isn't very meaningful information. *The meaningful information is when he looks at his cards early and then seems disinterested in the action.* Maybe he stares down towards his cards, or quickly glances at his phone, or looks at the tournament-status screen or the TV. These are hints that he's already mentally checked out of the hand.

This behavior *wouldn't* be meaningful if it were coming from a more recreational-level player, because those players are capable of acting disinterested when they have AA or KK, deceptively. This is only meaningful because it's a good player, and *good players generally want to pay attention to the situation when they have any sort of playable hand.* Mainly, though, it was meaningful because I'd seen it be reliable for that player multiple times.

This came into play in a few hands where I was in late position and this player was two seats behind me. Getting a sense that this player wasn't focused on the game encouraged me to make some raises I otherwise wouldn't have.

DANI STERN
on the importance of poker tells

Dani "The Real Ansky" Stern has been playing poker professionally since 2005. You may know him from his appearance on the TV shows *2 Months, $2 Million* and *PokerStars' The Big Game*. Recently, he was primarily playing mid- to high-stakes PLO online, with a few trips to big buy-in live tournaments and the WSOP. The following is from a talk we had in 2014.

ZACHARY ELWOOD: As someone who's played a lot live and online, what's your view on the importance of poker tells?

DANI STERN: Live, with regards to picking up physical tells or general demeanor from your opponents, I kind of think that the sky's the limit. You can always get better at it. There's always a lot of information to be gained.

Let's say, for example, somebody like Phil Ivey is the best in the world at picking up physical reads on opponents. That would give you such a tremendous edge. Like, if you know every time someone doesn't want you to reraise them. Or if you know every time when someone's looking for a call on the river.

I'm not saying that's what Phil Ivey is capable of; I don't think anyone is capable of knowing it every time. But it's just clearly something that can be very important. Getting a read on someone would allow you to play hands in ways that you just wouldn't normally be able to.

ELWOOD: How good, on a scale of 1 to 10, would you say you are at reading poker player behavior? Is it something you're always improving at?

STERN: I don't know: Six out of ten maybe. I guess I'm better than average. I don't think I'm great at it or anything. I think I've gotten better at it. It's not even like a conscious thing where I put work into it or study it; it's just as you get more experience it becomes intuitive and you get more of a feeling about what somebody's doing.

ELWOOD: Do you have any interesting anecdotes of recent hands where a player's behavior changed your decision?

STERN: I don't want to give away too much about specific players. But in general, with a lot of weak players, it's simpler than most people think. A lot of the times, strong means weak and weak means strong, just like the old classic Mike Caro information. I think it holds up pretty well, when you're talking about people who aren't aware of it and who don't play poker seriously. I'm pretty happy just using that concept alone for a lot of amateur players and it works out pretty well a lot of the time.

ELWOOD: It seems like bet-timing would be the only behavioral information you could get online. Would you say that's right?

STERN: When it comes to bet-timing, most people have that on lockdown. "I'm gonna wait just before the time bank runs out and bet" and they just do that every time, for every hand. So there's only so much information you can get.

ELWOOD: The immediate call seems to me to be the only bet-timing tell of much use online. When someone makes an immediate call in early parts of the hand, and the player isn't balanced, it's usually a medium-strength hand or draw, where they immediately ruled out raising. Compared to tanking a long time, which isn't as useful because someone could have just run to the bathroom or be doing something else online or whatever.

STERN: That fits with what I was saying before; strong means weak and weak means strong. They call quickly to show strength but really it just means they're weak. And as with all tells, you may be right, but you can only be partially right, you know? It doesn't mean it's a set-in-stone thing.

ELWOOD: It's a certain percentage of likelihood, right. How often, when you're playing with fairly decent players live, do you get a tell on someone that's very player-specific?

STERN: The "Oreo-cookie tell" is exceptionally rare in poker. *[Note: Stern is referencing Teddy KGB's tell in the movie Rounders.]* When you talk about reading people physically, it mostly means their breathing, their eye movement, if they're shaking, how they have their hands moving. How heavy they're breathing. What their posture is. Things like that.

I do know of a couple Oreo-cookie-type tells for opponents, but it's rare. If you see someone scratch their nose or whatever, you don't know if that means they're bluffing or value-betting so you still have to get to the river, see it happen, see the results, see it two or three other times, and confirm it and also see them not do it with the other strength hand.

So that's a pretty tough read, especially in a short period of time. But when you're playing someone over a long period of time, you can look for stuff like that. But for the most part, when people talk about tells, they're talking about the general energy someone's giving off. Comfortable or uncomfortable. Is he nervous? That type of thing.

Hand #12: Genuine indecision facing raise

$550 buy-in NLHE tournament

About ten hours into this tournament, most stacks were in the 15-20 BB range. The UTG+1 player had about 8 BBs and shoved.

The UTG+2 player had about 16 BBs and was a bad player. (He was the same player who said, "I'll just call," pre-flop with K♠ 9♣ in Hand #8.) After the player in front of him shoved, he immediately asked, "How much is it?" Then he looked back and forth from the all-in player to his chips. He started counting out his chips to see how much he had. His demeanor seemed uncertain.

I was immediately confident that this player was showing genuine indecision with a hand like AQs, JJ, or TT. I was confident that this was not a deceptive act with AA or KK. This player ended up calling and had AK offsuit, which is a little stronger than I thought he would be, but that was probably just a reflection of how tight and inexperienced he was.

You will sometimes see players, especially inexperienced players, putting on fake "indecisive" acts with AA or KK. So why was I so immediately certain that this player wasn't putting on an act?

The most important behavior here was his almost-immediate question, "How much is it?" This is a pretty reliable pattern that indicates a little bit of legitimate frustration and agitation. If this player had AA or KK, it's likely he would be a bit cagey and pause for a few seconds before doing anything. Players with strong hands don't like to draw attention to themselves, especially right after they look at a strong hand. So the immediate "How much is it?" is a clue that he's not super-strong and is actually frustrated, with an actual tough decision.

Another factor that increased my confidence in this read: *this player's seeming uncertainty was subtle*; it wasn't exaggerated like it might be if he were faking a tough decision with AA or KK. If he had put on more of a "show," shaking his head and acting sad about the situation, it would have started to seem more like deceptive behavior with a strong hand, which inexperienced players are capable of. But, as it was, *his behavior seemed like the genuine reaction of a fairly inexperienced player with a decent, medium-strength hand.*

What might be the practical benefit of understanding such a situation? If this player called, his behavior might encourage you to call or shove with some hands that you otherwise might be a little wary with. For example, if you were behind this player and had JJ, QQ, or AK, a shove and call from two early-position and tight players might make you a bit wary. Or the caller's behavior, if you thought it was a deceptive act with a strong hand, might spook you and get you to fold some strong hands. But knowing the caller's behavior is likely to be an honest display with a medium-strength hand, you could more comfortably call or shove with these hands.

Hand #13: Mentally unfocused statement when calling pre-flop

$1-2 NLHE cash game

A player limps early and the player behind him raises to $7. There are three calls and the early limper calls while saying, "You guys got me in. What are you guys doing?" He's laughing and smiling.

Let's examine this statement. For the most part, these kinds of statements will be said truthfully and indicate a weak range. High pairs have obviously become unlikely, because the player limped and then only called with so many other players in. But even hands like AJ, AT, KQ, and medium-pairs have become unlikely. It's pretty rare to see someone make statements like this with those types of decent, obviously-worth-a-call hands.

Later in the hand, the turn board is Q♣ T♥ 8♦ K♣. The player in question check-raises all-in for a large amount. His opponent debates a while, talking out loud about what his opponent might have. One of the things he says is, "I think you have Ace-Jack," and he eventually folds, showing J-9 for the low straight.

The all-in player then shows J-9, the same hand the player folded.

With our read on this player's pre-flop statement, it's unlikely he has AJ here. If you were his opponent and you were certain he had to have either AJ or J-9 to shove in this spot, his pre-flop statement would make it much more likely he had J-9. (His pre-flop statement also makes lots of other strong hands unlikely, like KQ, TT, and 88.)

This is just one example of how discounting certain hands can help you define an opponent's range on later streets.

Hand #14: Small movements when raising
$5-10 NLHE cash game

A tight player in early position raises to $20, but he does so with a lot of fits and starts in his movements. He gathers his raise then reaches for chips as if he's going to raise more, then finally puts in the raise with a quick movement.

Ostentatious behavior from pre-flop bettors and raisers makes it less likely they have QQ+. It's not nearly as reliable for bettors as it is for waiting-for-action players and non-aggressors, because players with strong hands are sometimes capable of all kinds of weird things just due to being relaxed, but it still will generally weaken a bettor's range. *Players with KK and AA, if they are the first-in raisers, will generally be inconspicuous and calm in their behavior.* The pot is small and these players have an instinct to not scare anyone away.

Note that this inconspicuous-behavior-when-betting-a-strong-hand tendency doesn't apply later in the hand. Later in the hand, bettors with strong hands can behave in conspicuous, ostentatious ways, for a few reasons: 1) the pot has become bigger and more worth winning as it is, 2) it is more obvious that the bettor is representing a strong hand and therefore there's less reason to attempt to be inconspicuous, 3) there's less mental focus required because the hand is close to being over, and 4) players confident of a win can be very relaxed, which leads to unusual, ostentatious behavior.

Back to the hand:

The tight player in early position has raised with a lot of fits and starts in his betting motion, making a strong hand less likely. One player in middle position calls the first player's raise.

I have 9♠ 8♠ on the button and I raise to $75. Both players call my raise and then fold to a bet on a T♦ 8♣ 5♠ flop.

Sometimes these small clues of ostentatious behavior from a raiser can encourage you to three-bet lighter than you normally would. But remember that these clues are still relatively small pieces of information that, pre-flop, will mainly make QQ+ less likely. These clues won't necessarily diminish the likelihood of hands like AK or JJ. Because it's a relatively small bit of information, other strategic factors should be favorable, too. To give one example: it helps to know that the first-in raiser has a fairly wide raising range. Another example: it helps if you know that your opponents, even if they call your three-bet, play fairly tight post-flop.

Hand #15: Unusual patience strengthens range

$1-2 NLHE cash game

There's a Mississippi straddle, where the player on the button puts up $5 and action starts on the small blind. Action gets paused on the small blind, who doesn't know it's his turn to act and is ordering food from the waitress.

The big blind has looked at his cards and, instead of telling the small blind to act, he sits there patiently and quietly for several seconds. After a long wait, the dealer eventually informs the SB that it's his turn.

At that moment, I thought it was very likely the BB had AA or KK. If he had a medium-strength or weak hand, he'd most likely let the SB know it was his action. He was a player I knew wasn't afraid to speak up.

Players with strong hands who are waiting for action to get to them generally don't want to draw attention to themselves. They will usually be patient and not want to rush an opponent's action.

The small blind calls and the big blind raises to $35. He turned out to have Q♦ Q♥.

Very infrequently, small clues can make you confident that a pre-flop raiser has QQ+. What's the practical benefit of making a read like this?

- If the player is loose and fairly deep, it'd be a good spot to call and try to make a hand on the flop, as you know that he'll usually be committing a good amount more chips.

- If the player is very tight and fairly deep, it might be a good spot to call with the intent of trying to take away the pot on scary boards.

- If the player is good or has a short stack, it's probably best to fold most hands, including most pairs. If the player is good, he's not going to be easy to outplay; knowing his probable range won't usually make up for him having such a head start on you. The short-stacked player doesn't have enough money to make calling pre-flop worthwhile; there's less to win if you do make a hand and it's more difficult to bluff.

It's important to note that folding medium-strength hands pre-flop is never that big a mistake. If you pick up a small clue of strength from an opponent early in a hand and it leads you to make a cautious fold, you won't be making that big of an error even if you're wrong in that specific hand.

Hand #16: Ostentatious bet motions from raiser
$2-5 NLHE cash game

In middle position, I raise to $15 with A♣ K♥.

The button is a loose but fairly passive player. After my raise, he looks at his cards and quickly and agitatedly makes it $40. He immediately reaches for chips and throws them into the pot with a good amount of force, and with a good amount of unnecessary movement.

As with other ostentatious behavior early in a hand, this makes AA and KK less likely than it would otherwise be. (Plus, my own AK makes those hands less likely.)

Action comes back to me and I make it $130, ready to call a shove (he has about $500). After 30 seconds he folds, saying, "If I can't fold ace-king, I can't play this game."

Immediate raises can be another small clue to a player

not having the very top of their range. (This is generally reliable pre-flop, but it becomes less reliable after the flop, where things get more complicated.)

Hand #17: A snap-shove with AK

Poker After Dark, Season 5

In this episode of *Poker After Dark*, they played a winner-take-all cash game freeze-out: essentially a tournament but played cash-game style.

Phil Gordon raises to $1,200 UTG with A♣ K♦. Right behind him, Gabe Kaplan makes it $6,200 with Q♦ Q♥.

Everyone folds and action returns to Gordon. He immediately says, "I'm all-in" for $20,350.

Kaplan thinks for quite a long time and eventually folds.

Phil Hellmuth says, "Ace-king I thought maybe Phil Gordon had. Because he reraised so quickly. If he had aces or kings he might have hemmed and hawed a little bit, I thought."

Hellmuth's point: *It's common for players with AA or KK to put on a little act of indecision before raising or shoving pre-flop.* This indecisive act might be an actual verbal act (literal 'hemming and hawing'), it might be physical indicators of indecision (a pained grimace or shaking of the head, for example), or it might just be pausing a while before acting.

Hellmuth's read was also based on the fact that he knew Phil Gordon was a tight, disciplined player. He knew Gordon well enough to know he wasn't shoving very light. If Hellmuth could reduce Gordon's shoving range to something like AK, AQ and TT+, and if Gordon's immediate shove made KK/AA very unlikely (with AQ, TT, and JJ also unlikely because

Gordon would probably think a little first), then AK is the only remaining snap-shoving hand.

(Worth noting: assuming the displayed stack sizes were correct on the show, this should have been a mandatory call for Kaplan.)

Hand #18: Snap-raise weakens range

$550 buy-in NLHE tournament

It's a few hours into this tournament and I have about 50 BBs. I have T♠ T♦ in the cutoff. It's folded to the player in front of me, who looks at his cards and *immediately* raises from 500 to 1600.

This player has me covered. He's a tight player and so I'd usually be cautious and just call. But his speed of raising makes it likely he doesn't have the very top of his range, so I three-bet to 5000. He calls.

On a flop of A♠ K♦ 3♦ he bets 5000 and I fold.

Hand #19: Obstacles to action weaken range

$1-2 NLHE cash game

The button puts up $5 on the button for the Mississippi straddle. He's a regular who I play $2-5 and $5-10 with fairly often. He's mostly straightforward in his play and not often aggressive.

Action is on me in the small blind. I have J♦ J♣ and make it $15. There's one caller in middle position.

I jokingly say, "You gotta call" to the button straddler as he looks at his cards. The dealer reprimands me, telling me not to influence action. (In most cash games, this kind of joking behavior, especially pre-flop, rarely bothers anyone.) I jokingly follow up by telling the straddler, "Sorry, you gotta *raise*."

The straddler fairly quickly makes it $55. He mumbles something about "having a raising hand."

Both the speed of his raise after looking (less than two seconds) and his talking make me think it's unlikely he has QQ+. With QQ or better I think it's likely he'd both:

- Be more mentally focused, and hence more quiet

- Take a little longer to act, in order to not seem so certain

From my knowledge of his play, I also think it's unlikely he'd raise so quickly with JJ (plus I have JJ) or lower pairs, or AQ. For all of these reasons, it's very likely he has AK. I know from playing with him that he will usually fold AK to a four-bet.

Another player, who's out of the hand, jokingly says, "See what you did?" to me, implying that I'd encouraged the straddler to raise.

The straddler says quietly, "That's not why."

The straddler has made two strong-hand statements; in other words, his statements imply, however subtly, that he has a strong hand. With the last statement, the subtext is: "I'm not raising because of anything someone said; I'm raising because I have a strong hand."

I think it's unlikely he'd make these statements with AA or KK, because he wouldn't want to discourage action, however subtly. He's not a verbally tricky guy, so I think it's very unlikely he'd be making these statements with AA or KK as some kind of tricky false tell. I think it's possible but unlikely he'd behave this way with QQ. The most likely hand by far, though, is AK.

Both the straddler and I had about $300 to start the hand. I raise to $150. I predict that he'll most likely fold AK, but there's a decent chance—because it's lower-stakes than we both usually play—that he'll decide to shove. If he does end up shoving, I'm obviously calling.

As it turns out, I get a call from the middle-position player, who has $150; he has 55. The straddler folds what he later tells me was AK.

Some players, especially at lower limits, will never be folding AK pre-flop. Let's say you were up against a player in a similar situation and you were pretty sure of both these things:

- His style and behavior make AK very likely
- He will never be folding AK pre-flop

In that case, your best strategy might be to just call your opponent's three-bet, see if the flop brings an Ace or a King, and play it accordingly from there. This would avoid the variance of a close all-in pre-flop situation (~55% for JJ, 45% for AK, and it's actually a bit worse for you than that because your opponent will still, even with a solid read, sometimes have QQ+).

Hand #20: Raiser slams chips, announces raise loudly

$2-5 NLHE cash game

It's a loose, passive game without much pre-flop raising. There's a $10 straddle UTG. I limp UTG+1 with K♥ T♥.

There are two other calls and then a loose-aggressive

young guy quickly and loudly announces "One hundred." He puts in a stack for a raise to $100, slamming the chips in pretty forcefully. Action comes back to me and as I think, the raiser is moving around, touching his chips, and looking towards me a good amount.

All of these ostentatious behaviors make me think he's not focused, as he probably would be with a strong hand. (Again, this is an early-hand pattern; if this player were acting this way on the river when betting, it'd be a different situation and be likely to indicate relaxation.) The bet-sizing is also a factor here; it's hard to imagine him raising that big if he actually wanted action.

I have about $800 and this player has me covered.

One reason I sometimes limp early first-in is so I can represent AA or KK if the situation seems right. I make it $300. Everyone folds, including him: he shows 7♠ 2♥.

The bet-sizing is meaningful here, but if it were just the sizing alone, I wouldn't have acted on it, because it's fairly common for a player to make a large raise with TT, JJ, or QQ, and be committed to more action. Also, the sizing isn't super-reliable because some scared-money players like to just take down the pot with AA or KK.

Hand #21: Raiser reaches for chips early

$1-2 NLHE cash game

A player limps early. I have 9♠ 7♠ in late position. I go to call but before I even begin to put in chips, I see a tight and predictable player behind me putting together chips for a raise. I call and this player raises to $12.

Reaching for chips out-of-turn makes a very strong hand

unlikely. If this player had KK or AA, he'd be mentally focused and he wouldn't want to intimidate the players in front of him out of calling or raising.

I also know that this player often limps with JJ and TT. This makes it even more likely that he has AK/AQ-type hands here.

Everyone folds back to me. Without the behavioral information, I'd be folding. But because I put him on a weaker range, I call. I can either flop a pair that's likely to be good, or I can outplay him if he shows weakness later in the hand (e.g., checking back the turn). Part of my reason for wanting to play with this player here is that he's predictable; if he were unpredictable, I'd have less reason to want to go uphill against a stronger range.

You might be wondering: if I'm so sure he's on the weaker side, why not three-bet him?

While I think that a three-bet would often be successful and take down the pot, the problem with that approach is that, if your opponent is at all decent, he'll realize you're not logically representing much of a hand yourself. By you just limping after another limper, it's become much less likely you have a big hand, and there's a chance this fact will encourage an opponent to call you or four-bet you with hands like AK, AQ, and medium pairs. (If you were the first-in early limper, the limp-reraise becomes more defensible, as more people will give you credit for playing AA/KK like that.)

This comes up a lot when trying to make use of tells: *even when an opponent's range might seem weak to you based on their behavior, you also have to take into account how your range looks to them.*

Hand #22: Long initial looks at hole cards
$100 buy-in NLHE tournament

In a 50-person $100 buy-in tournament, I'm heads-up with an inexperienced young player. Since we've been four-handed, I've noticed he has a very prominent, reliable tell when he does his initial look at his hole cards:

- If he stares at his cards for a second or two, he is *very unlikely* to have a strong hand. (While one second doesn't sound like a long time, it is long compared to most looks, which are a half-second or less.)

- When he puts his hole cards down immediately after his initial look, he is *a bit more likely* to have a strong hand.

This is a common and reliable pattern for amateur players and it's worth understanding exactly why and how this pattern shows up.

First let's look at the general psychological motivations behind quick looks and long looks:

For strong hands:

- A player who looks down at a strong hand has an instinct to not draw attention to his "treasure." In my first book, I compared it to a scene in the movie *Blood Diamond* where the main character, who is forced to work at a diamond mine, finds a large diamond. His captors are nearby, and he immediately averts his eyes, looking somewhere else, attempting to look nonchalant. The audience knows immediately that he is thinking of keeping the diamond for himself and that he doesn't want his enemies to know where his attention has been drawn. This is instinctual behavior, and it applies to amateur players who look down at very strong hands.

- Players who look down at strong hands may want to put the cards down quickly so as to avoid someone nearby seeing their hand.

Another minor factor: strong hands are easily understood visually and require less actual studying to make sense of. For example: pocket pairs are immediately comprehended, and their suits are less important, while a hand like 9-7 will take slightly longer to fully recognize and to see what the suits are. Offsuit, non-paired hands can require more studying, due to being harder to parse visually. They can also take slightly more actual thought on how to play, which can lead to slightly longer stares. These are minor factors, but they contribute.

For weak and medium-strength hands:

- Players who look down at weak or medium-strength hands don't have a reason to look away. Long looks at hole cards can mainly be understood as simply the lack of a reason to look away.

- Players who stare at weak hole cards may have an instinct to express interest in their cards.

- As stated, weak or medium-strength hands are harder to parse visually, can require more thought on how to play, and require more effort to remember.

This is not much of a factor in Hold'em, but it is more of a factor in games with more hole cards, like Omaha or 5-card-draw. In those cases, long stares at cards can be reliable signs that a player is likely actually studying the hand and doesn't have an easily understood (strong) hand.

These are the dominant psychological factors behind the pattern, but in practice it's not as straightforward as: "Quick looks are strong hands, long looks are weak hands." *Rather, in practice, long looks at hole cards contain much more information than quick looks at hole cards and are much more useful.*

Why is this? It's because looking at cards quickly is the usual way to look at cards. Most people, in general, will glance at their hole cards quickly, whether they have a strong or weak hand. Because of this, quick looks have less meaning. There is some meaning, because a good percentage of weak hands will be long looks, which leaves more strong hands in the quick-look category. This is why I say quick looks make strong hands *a bit more likely*, but not *very likely*.

Long looks, however, are less common, and they are highly correlated to being weak or medium-strength. It is quite rare for amateur players to stare for a second or two at hands like JJ+ or AK. This is more practical and actionable information than is the quick look.

Some players, of course, don't abide by these patterns. Some people are consistent in how long they look at their cards. Some people do the opposite of the general pattern. As with all tells, you'll ideally be watching someone for a little while to see if the pattern applies to them before basing decisions on it.

Back to the heads-up match against the kid with the reliable long-look tell:

Heads-up is the perfect scenario for making use of such a tell. At a full table, this tell is of limited use because you'll have so few opportunities to make use of it versus the specific player you noticed displaying it. But heads-up, you can act on it frequently.

When we started heads-up I had about 30 BBs and he had 100 BBs. He was obviously inexperienced at heads-up play; while he was capable of fairly frequent pre-flop raises, he was too tight otherwise, so my shoves had a lot of fold equity.

My general strategy was as follows:

- If he stared for a second or two at his cards and then raised, and I had weak and medium-strength hands (including QQ and AK) I would shove (or raise if my stack was big enough). I'd fold the super-weak hands as I did want some equity if called and I also didn't want to be so frequently aggressive that he would adjust. (Also remember that the long look mainly makes strong hands unlikely; it's still easily possible he has a hand like AQ or AJs or a medium-pair and finds a call.)

- If he stared for a second or two at his cards and raised, and I had AA or KK, I would only call.

- If he stared for a second or two and just called, I'd make larger raises with weaker hands and smaller raises with strong hands. (Because he was inexperienced I wasn't worried about him exploiting that strategy in the short-term.)

- When he looked quickly at his hole cards, I'd play more straightforwardly but err on the side of caution. For example, if I was on the fence about whether to call or fold, I'd opt to fold. If I was on the fence about three-betting or calling, I'd opt to call.

Basically my goal was to focus on getting folds when I saw him do a long look. That happened pretty often: every few hands. The read was reliable and was a big edge, so I just focused on winning hands that way, and hardly played any hands post-flop.

I fairly quickly gained the chip lead and ended up winning the tournament (not that that means anything, but it was a nice outcome).

Hand #23: Long pause before shoving short stack
$1-2 NLHE cash game

I raise to $7 in middle position with 9♠ 9♥.

A young guy, who only has $40, starts to stack up chips, as if thinking about calling or raising. After about 8 seconds, he shoves for $40.

Action returns to me. I ask him, "What you got?"

He laughs and says, "I only got a few chips."

I fold and he shows K♥ K♠. Assuming this player is always shoving with AK and AQ with such a short stack (which I believe he is), this is mathematically a clear call for me. But when you factor in that most players with only $40 will be shoving quickly with AK, AQ, and medium pairs, his hesitation makes it a bit more likely that he's putting on a deceptive act with a strong hand.

Worth mentioning here: *the main reason his pausing here is useful is because he is so short-stacked.* If he had a normal-sized stack, his pausing wouldn't be meaningful (unless it was a very excessive pause). Immediate bets and raises will often contain some meaning, but assuming normal stacks, a few seconds of thinking isn't going to be meaningful, because most people in most situations think a little bit before acting. (In other words, the absence of a tell is not necessarily a tell.)

But with short stacks in such a spot, where AK and AQ and medium-sized pairs will be more obviously "no-brainer" shoves, hesitation becomes more meaningful.

Also, his relaxed laughing and his statement downplaying his stack size make it a bit more likely he's relaxed and would like a call. Although on their own I wouldn't read much into either of those behaviors in this spot, as that behavior can vary a lot, especially in low-pressure situations.

Hand #24: Shover's ostentatious behavior weakens range
$1-2 NLHE cash game

A loose player straddles UTG for $5.

I make it $20 with A♦ Q♠ and get one caller behind me.

The straddler shoves immediately for $120, with a lot of force, saying with a smile, "Okay, let's go!"

This player is definitely capable of occasionally shoving here with a fairly wide range, but I still think, not taking into account his behavior, he'll usually have something pretty strong. Calling here feels like a pretty break-even proposition, especially when taking into account there is still a player behind me.

But his immediate shove, his ostentatious behavior, and his smile make the strongest hands (~QQ+) less likely. With those hands, because the pot is small, I think he'd not want to set up any obstacles to action, plus I think he'd be more focused.

I also think it makes AK a little bit less likely than usual, as he'd often be more mentally focused, and silent, with AK. To be clear: I don't think his behavior makes AK that unlikely; I wouldn't be surprised to see AK here. It just increases the chances that he's shoving fairly light.

Believing that his hand range is weaker than usual makes this an easier call. There are a lot of borderline spots like this that come up, especially in games where people are short-stacked, and I often use opponent behavior as a deciding factor if I'm on the fence.

I call. He had A♣ T♣.

Hand #25: Raiser's question weakens range

$5-10 NLHE cash game

The UTG player raises to $35. I call in late position with A♥ T♥.

Before the flop comes out, the raiser says to me, "You just playing a rush? Or do you have a legitimate hand?"

Early in a hand, players with the strongest hands (QQ+) generally will be focused and thoughtful. They want to think about the best way to play the hand and they want to think about the situation. Also, with these strong hands, these players generally have an instinct not to draw attention to themselves.

Most of these kinds of situations, where the raiser talks after being called, will indicate a player with a weak or medium-strength hand. I talked about this pattern in my book *Verbal Poker Tells*. Sometimes this pattern shows up when a player raises, gets multiple calls, and says something jokingly about how much action he's getting. It's rare for a player with KK or AA to make comments in these situations.

For a lot of this kind of talking from pre-flop raisers, it will indicate that they are planning on playing the hand straightforwardly and not planning on continuing to bet without improvement. This verbal behavior can be seen as a release of tension, of breaking focus and taking off their "game face."

Knowing that these kinds of statements have made AA and KK less likely can help narrow down your average early-position raiser's range to just a few hands, many of them being AK. This can encourage you to float some flops you otherwise wouldn't, hoping to take the pot away on the turn. Or it can encourage you to bluff if the flop appears to help your range more than his.

Back to the hand: the flop comes 8♦ 7♠ 5♣. The pre-flop raiser bets $40. I raise to $120 with my A♥ T♥ and he folds.

Hand #26: Caller's statement contains clues
$2-5 NLHE cash game

There are two limps and I limp in late position with 9♣ 8♣.

A player calls on the button and says, "Okay, put out some garbage and I'll be right in the middle of it."

While these kinds of statements will often be said slightly truthfully with weaker hands, *when a player says that his hand is "garbage," it will usually not actually be garbage.* It'll often be a pretty weak hand of some sort, like Q5s or 86o, but it won't usually be two weak cards (like 5-2, 6-3, or 7-2).

This kind of statement also makes a lot of stronger hands (pocket pairs, strong aces) less likely, because *with stronger hands players are typically more focused and therefore more silent.* Another contributing reason: *players with decent hands, like pocket pairs, generally don't like to lie in such direct ways.*

The flop is 7♥ 3♥ 3♦. There are a few checks and I bet $15 into $25. Only the button calls.

This is interesting because even though his range calling the button after several limps is quite wide, and even though he implied he wanted "garbage," his pre-flop statement makes actual "garbage" less likely. In other words, it's a bit less likely than usual that he has a 3. It's of course possible he has a 3, but other hands, like a 7 or a flush draw, have become more likely than usual.

Also, 77 is less likely than usual because, like I said, players with pocket pairs don't like to make direct lies, like calling their hand garbage pre-flop.

The turn is a Q♣.

I bet $30 into $55. If it weren't for his pre-flop statement, I'd probably check. He calls.

The river is the A♦. I like this because I think with his pre-flop statement he'll usually not have an Ace (again owing to most people's honesty with such statements). I bluff $80 into $115. He thinks for a while and calls with Q♥ T♥: he'd flopped the flush draw but hit the Queen on the turn.

2013 WSOP Main Event final table analysis

Leading up to the 2013 World Series of Poker Main Event final table, I consulted for Amir Lehavot, who would go on to get 3rd place in that year's event.

My job involved going through the existing ESPN footage for that event and other footage from other events Amir's opponents had played in, looking for behavioral patterns.

I won't lie to you: it's hard to find something in these circumstances, for a few reasons:

- These days, most of the Main Event final table players are professional-caliber.

- The sample size is pretty small; there aren't that many hands to study in the existing footage or during the final table itself.

- The players have several months to prepare for the final table, and they are typically focused on being as stoic and unreadable as possible.

- Most of the action at the final table takes place pre-flop, where hand strength is undefined and it's hard to get reliable reads.

It's definitely *possible* to find reliable patterns—I've found a very reliable tell on a WSOP Main Event champion before—it's just understandably uncommon. Considering the money on the line, though, it can be worthwhile to look for patterns.

That year, the player who I was most confident of finding something interesting on was Sylvain Loosli. Loosli was a French player who'd played a lot online but who hadn't played much live. In the footage leading up to the final table, he was full of a lot of diverse physical behavior: moving around a lot, a lot of hand motions, a lot of chip handling motions, etc.

One hypothesis I had about him was that he had more pauses in his chip-gathering movements and pauses before betting or raising when he had a strong hand. When he was betting or raising with weaker hands or bluffs, his movements tended to be more straightforward, more efficient, but with stronger hands, there was a lot more "unnecessary" movements and hesitation involved.

The explanation for this behavior (if it was indeed a pattern for him) is a simple and common one: *players with weaker hands want to place their bets in a fairly normal, straightforward manner.* They don't want to be studied any longer than they have to be. And they want to convey (even subconsciously) some confidence. Players with strong hands are more relaxed and their bet-gathering can be more meandering and take longer. They don't care as much about being studied and they may even have a motivation to appear uncertain.

This idea seemed to hold up after watching his play at the final table. A few examples:

With QQ: After he puts a chip on his cards, making it evident he's most probably going to raise, he pauses for a couple seconds, flipping chips, before he starts to assemble a raise.

With KK: After he puts a chip on his cards and it's evident he's probably going to be raising, he again just pauses for a couple seconds, flipping chips, before reaching for chips.

With KK again: He puts a chip on his cards, then he just sits there for almost ten seconds before raising.

After limping with AA: After being checked to on the flop, he brings his hand down from his face and looks down at his chips, making it very likely he's going to be betting. Then he just shuffles chips for a few seconds before reaching for a bet.

Compared to the spots where he raised pre-flop or bet post-flop with weak hands, there are a lot more pauses in the hands above. There were times where he put in bets and raises very straightforwardly with strong hands, too, but the point is that *the pauses and unnecessary movements seemed to increase the likelihood that he was strong.*

The practical upshot of this would be that if you were on the fence about what to do facing a raise from Loosli (whether to fold, call, or three-bet), and his raising behavior had some hesitations in it, you'd take a more cautious approach. If you were going to call his raise or make a light three-bet, you'd rather do it when his raise behavior seemed more normal and straightforward.

Again, in Loosli's defense: I wasn't *certain* this was a pattern for him. The sample size was still small. But I was confident it was a pattern for him, as it does fit a fairly common behavioral pattern.

If you want to check it out for yourself, you can watch a compilation video I made of Loosli's final table play. It's on YouTube; do a web search for 'Sylvain Loosli final table compilation' and you should be able to find it. When you've found the video, you might like to subscribe to my YouTube channel and check out my other videos.

Hand #27: Chip handling tells influence a decision
2015 European Poker Tour €5,300 buy-in NLHE tournament

PokerStars.com's blog published the following tournament hand where Dominik Panka, a professional poker player, made an impressive pre-flop fold with TT. The tournament was down to only 3 players: this is why Panka's fold is impressive.

Valentin Messina is on the button and raises to 325K. Panka has 4.6M: he three-bets to 850K with TT. Jean Montury has 4.6M: he four-bets to 2.1M. Messina folds and action is back on Panka.

Panka describes the reasons behind his decision to fold:

> It's a really interesting hand, I pick up tens in the small blind and Valentin opened from the button. He was opening super wide, some hands he folded because I played with Jean blind versus blind many times, but sometimes he opened 7-2 off so his opening range is very wide. So for me it's a great spot to three-bet against him and get it in. But Jean makes a large four-bet and he's playing very snug.
>
> I'd got a lot of information from my friends watching the feed about the way he plays and the way he was acting during hands, as he gives off a decent amount of tells. I'm not an expert with tells but we were pretty quickly able to identify that how he touches and moves his chips depends on the strength of his hand. If he had a decent hand but he wasn't really comfortable with it then he was stroking his chips. But, if he had a good hand he was either shuffling his chips or moving them in a different way.
>
> Additionally he was raising smaller with weaker hands. If he had Ace-Queen or nines here he would probably have raised to around 1,600,000. So, he pretty quickly gave away

the strength of his hand. Obviously he can have Ace-King there but I was pretty comfortable with this fold. In other circumstances against other players, TT 3-handed with 30 big blinds is a premium hand and you get it in.

I also knew that even though I was quite short I had a decent shot if I doubled up. So I also considered tournament life and the fact that I think I am the most experienced and that Valentin was the tougher opponent and Jean was playing pretty straight-forward. This wasn't his first four-bet though, he had four-bet with Ace-King, but bigger and quicker.

I had a very good read on him and I was pretty comfortable folding tens. I don't think I would've laid QQ down, I would never have forgiven myself if he had a worse hand. I would probably have got it in with JJ and AK suited. Fortunately I had the tens.

Hand #28: Quick call of four-bet defines range
$5-10 NLHE cash game

I raise in middle position with K♣ K♦ to $35. A fairly tight player behind me makes it $115. Stacks are $1,200. I make it $325 and my opponent calls after three seconds.

This situation comes up fairly frequently: an opponent calling a three-bet or four-bet quickly. This might be a literal "snap call," or it might just be an unusually fast call considering a player's usual speed of action. In most of these cases, these quick calls will point to medium-strength hands: hands that, from that player's perspective, are obviously too strong to fold, while also obviously too weak to raise.

For most recreational players, quick-calls of pre-flop three-bets and four-bets will make JJ and QQ likely. JJ is signifi-cantly more likely than QQ, but QQ becomes more likely the tighter the player is. (Some inexperienced players may also call quickly with AK, whereas better players will usually spend a little time thinking about the situation before reaching a decision.) How well you're able to pinpoint a player's range will depend on your knowledge of their playing style.

In this case, because I had a few dozen hours playing with this player, I was very confident he had QQ. I knew he was tight enough that he would probably at least consider folding JJ and AK. I knew if he had AA or KK he would consider raising. So there wasn't much left except QQ.

Knowing that AA, KK, and AK are unlikely is obviously great information to have post-flop. It can influence you to bluff on Ace-high boards, and it can encourage you to slowplay if you think that you're ahead but your opponent will fold to a bet.

Worth mentioning here: *quick calls and quick bets are basically the only possible tells you might find when playing online poker.* Unlike long pauses before calling or betting, a quick call cannot be faked. Unless a player always acts very quickly, it's likely a quick call or a quick bet contains some meaning. This is not true with bets or checks that take an abnormally long time; online, there are many factors that could lead to a delay, such as multi-tabling, a bathroom break, or other distractions.

Hand #29: A snap-call of a three-bet
$5-10 NLHE cash game

A very tight player makes it $35 in the hijack. And "very tight" is an understatement: this guy is probably one of the tightest players in the world. It's basically impossible to get value out of him, so my only approach when in hands with him is to try to get him off hands whenever I see a promising spot to do so.

He has about $700 to start this hand and I cover.

When this player raises pre-flop, it's a very tight range. He often doesn't raise first-in with AK, but he will in late position. I've noticed that when he raises late with hands like AK or AQ or low pairs, he makes his raises larger than he would if he had big pairs. If he had KK or AA, he'd probably make it $30 here, so his $35 raise makes KK and AA less likely.

A player behind him calls; this player is fairly tight and mostly straightforward. I'm in the big blind with K♦ 8♦. I make it $135.

I know that if the first raiser has AA or KK, he will be waiting a while and then either shoving or near-shoving. If he has AK or pairs JJ or lower, he'll most likely be folding. The only hands he'll just call with, I think, are QQ, and maybe JJ and AKs.

He calls my raise after only about three seconds. This quick call—quick when taking into account his usual behavior—restricts this player almost exclusively to QQ. If he had paused a bit before putting in the call, it becomes more possible he might have JJ or AKs, but the immediate call is very range-defining for a player this tight.

The other player calls also.

The flop is K♣ Q♥ 7♦. I check and the tight player bets $300 into $420. The other player folds and I fold.

The bettor shows Q♦ Q♣, for a set.

Even if I had a strong hand here on this flop, including AA or a set of 7s, I would have folded to any bet from him.

That's how confident I was that his behavior combined with his playing style narrowed his range to only QQ.

Hand #30: Agitated question before calling raise
$2-5 NLHE cash game

A player in late position, who's pretty tight and predictable, raises to $20. He has about $500.

I'm on the button with 4♣ 4♦ and make it $65.

Action gets back to him and he immediately says, kind of agitatedly, "How much is it?" After a few seconds, he calls.

We talked about this earlier: this kind of immediate question, especially when it seems on the more frustrated side, makes very strong hands (pre-flop, mainly AA and KK) unlikely, while also making it likely he's got something decently strong.

For this player, with this behavior and with this call, I think it's likely he has a hand like JJ or TT; these are hands that many players won't fold pre-flop but that also stress them out. I think if this player had QQ or AK, he'd usually be more thoughtful and wouldn't immediately act agitated like that.

The flop is A♣ 9♥ 5♥. He checks, I bet $75, and he calls fairly quickly.

Quick calls are likely to be medium-strength hands. With AK and AQ, I think he'd at least consider a raise (and I don't see him calling with worse aces pre-flop) so I'm still confident he's got a hand like JJ, TT, maybe QQ. 99 is theoretically in his range but it's now unlikely because with such a draw-heavy board, most people with a set will at least be considering a raise here.

The turn is another 5. He checks and I bet $170. He folds. Without the behavioral clues in this hand, I would have probably taken a less aggressive approach.

Hand #31: Last-second attempt to discourage a call
Seminole Hard Rock Poker Open, $5K buy-in NLHE tournament

The following is a hand submitted by semi-pro player Corey Hochman, a regular in high buy-in tournaments:

> Let's set the stage. There are 12 players left at the Seminole Hard Rock Poker Open (SHRPO) $5K buy-in Main Event. I'm one of them. The average chip count is about 1.7M and I'm sitting on 2.0M. We're at two six-handed tables. Pro player Zo Karim is the short stack at my table with 800K and he's been very active.
>
> I wake up with AT suited and limp for 60K under-the-gun. Zo insta-shoves for 800K. An insta-shove is polarizing: usually it's pretty strong or else weak. It folds back to me. I'm probably folding, but want to think about it for a minute.
>
> I say, "Zo, I'm like 99% certain I have you beat and I'm probably calling. Just need a minute to think." He sits silently. I have no read on him. I think for a minute and am ready to fold.
>
> I reach into my stack and grab the bet amount and carefully place those chips to the side of my stack, measuring them out, like you usually see before someone calls.
>
> Zo sees me counting out chips and blurts out, "So you're calling, right?"
>
> If Zo is polarized with the insta-shove, then this comment is usually going to indicate weakness. He thinks I'm going to call and is trying something to make me reconsider. If he had a very

strong hand, he'd probably keep his mouth shut.

So I've gone from 100% folding to 100% calling. I make the call. He shows Q-T, spikes a Queen, and doubles up on me. Oh well.

Thoughts from Zach: I like the general idea here. It's true that players who see you preparing to call and who do something unusual will generally not want the call and are attempting some last-second discouragement.

At the same time, I think it's entirely possible Zo acts this way with AK-AJ here, as most people are quite content just taking down the pot in such spots and not facing a race. But yes, this combination of behaviors makes it more likely a player is on the weaker side.

I think it's probable that Zo, being experienced, knows the general meaning of these behaviors and was attempting to manipulate a player he viewed as an amateur. In other words, *he thought it was more likely Corey would be discouraged from calling than it was that Corey would interpret his behavior as weakness*. I think it's likely if Zo believed his opponent were experienced, he wouldn't have attempted such a thing.

Flop and Turn Tells

Hand strength becomes more defined on the flop, although with two cards to come there's still a lot of ambiguity and ambivalence.

On the flop, it's possible to have strong but vulnerable made hands, as well as strong draws. For example: a player with an overpair to the flop might feel very vulnerable, even if they're willing to put in a lot of money. In the same way, a player with a strong draw might feel very relaxed and also be willing to put in a lot of money.

For these reasons, reliable reads are rare on the flop. But there are occasional small clues that make weakness or strength more likely. Similar to pre-flop clues, these can sometimes be useful for changing a decision in a borderline spot. Board texture will also play a big role in how actionable these tells are.

Hand strength becomes more defined on the turn. With one card to come, it becomes much harder to have a draw that's ahead of a made hand, so tells of weakness or strength, especially from bettors, become more common and reliable.

Hand #32: Pause before check indicates interest
$1-2 NLHE cash game

I raise to $7 in late position with J♥ T♥. The big blind calls. He's a bad, loose-aggressive player. He has about $200.

The flop is Q♦ 7♣ 5♣. The BB takes about five seconds to check. This is unusual behavior for him; he usually acts pretty quickly—within a few seconds—in normal, non-big-bet spots.

A long pause before checking, in general, will make it unlikely that a player has a strong hand. If a player has a very strong hand and decides to check it, he has an incentive to check quickly, so as not to "get in the way" of an opponent continuing to bet. Taking a weirdly long time to check could theoretically make an opponent wary, and a player with a strong hand doesn't want that. In most cases, long pauses will indicate defensiveness and are meant to communicate, "I'm interested in this hand so be careful."

But most long pauses before checking will be useful later in a hand, when a player's hand strength is a little better defined based on how he's played the hand. For example, an abnormally long pause before checking the river is almost always defensive when done by recreational players.

In this early-hand situation, while this player's behavior is likely to represent a weak hand, *it also indicates interest in the hand and actually strengthens this player's range*. In other words: the pause makes it more likely that the player has connected to this flop in some way, however weakly. Put another way: if this player completely missed the flop, he'd probably just be checking quickly and folding.

Maybe he has a weak Queen, maybe he has a low pair,

maybe he has a flush draw, maybe he has a straight draw; the point is that the pause indicates some sort of hand. (I think hands like gut-shot straight draws are quite common in this kind of situation, just because it's a hand that is more likely to make a player think a few seconds, compared to other, more quickly understood hands and draws.)

Because this player is loose and aggressive, it's very likely that he's going to at least call a flop bet. He may even raise the flop. It would be unusual for a somewhat experienced loose player to pause for such a long time, expressing interest in the hand, and end up folding.

This is a great flop to c-bet, in a vacuum. But considering this player's behavior and tendencies, I check back here. I think this player has interest in the hand and I know he likes to call; that's not a good combination. I'm willing to get more involved if I improve or if a good scare card (Ace or King) comes, but otherwise I'm pretty done with the hand.

Let's imagine this same behavior came from a pretty tight player, though. If this opponent were tight, I would always bet this flop and continue to bet the turn and maybe the river, unless something happens that changes my mind. Because the pause-check behavior still makes the strongest hands less likely, I'm confident I'll usually be getting folds from tight players, even if it means I have to bluff all three streets occasionally. It's also a good spot because, with the flush draw out there, most players with strong hands will be raising the flop or the turn, so I'll find out where I'm at if they have their strongest hands, limiting my losses when I'm bluffing.

Checking back the flop in this situation may seem very

weak, but against loose players who call or bet too much, your main goal is to make hands against them. Continuation-betting weak hands against loose, aggressive players is a pretty borderline situation to begin with. Considering it's borderline, it's justifiable to use a small clue to err on the more cautious side.

Again: A pause before checking is only meaningful if that behavior is unusual for that player. If a player regularly takes a long time to check to you, the behavior has lost its meaning. But many players will tend to check quickly when they're not interested, and for those players, pauses can indicate some actual thought.

Hand #33: Analyzing a verbal call-for-a-card

$1-2 NLHE cash game

I raise pre-flop to $8 with A♦ Q♣ and get two callers. The caller in the big blind yells, "Eight!", requesting an 8 on the flop.

How this pattern often shows up is with some indirect truth. It's likely that an 8 will actually help his hand, but in an indirect way. So it's unlikely he has 88, or A-8 or 9-8. It'll usually be something like 9-7, or maybe 7-6, because with those hands an 8 would get him closer to a straight.

The flop comes K♣ Q♠ 8♥. The player is laughing and saying, "I asked for an eight!" and double-checking his cards. His double-checking of cards, because it's ostentatious and from a waiting-to-act player, makes a strong hand unlikely.

Same for him drawing attention to the flop: players who draw attention to the board, especially right after new cards come out, are likely to be weak. *Players who flop well don't like to draw attention to the situation.* If they say something about the board, it'll often be after a few seconds and not immediately; in the first few seconds, they will tend to instinctually be more cagey and silent.

(In this situation, this verbal behavior on the flop isn't very meaningful, just because his call for an eight makes it more likely he'll continue talking post-flop when an eight comes.)

I bet and the two opponents fold. I ask the player what he had and he says he had T-7.

Sometimes player's pre-flop calls-for-cards may seem silly and meaningless but can help you narrow down a player's range, and this will occasionally help you later in the hand.

Hand #34: Aggressive check weakens range
$2-5 NLHE cash game

There is one early limp and I limp on the button with A♥ 4♦. With the big blind, we go three-way to a flop of T♦ T♣ 8♠.

The big blind checks by making a hard slam with his hand on the table. The second guy also checks with a slam of his hand. He also moves around a lot in his seat and sits staring at the board.

Similar to pre-flop clues, these kinds of ostentatious behaviors make it less likely these players have a ten here. If they had flopped trips or better, they'd likely be gentler in their mannerisms.

Also, the second player's staring-at-the-board is likely to indicate a weak hand. When players flop very well, they will generally look away from the flop, at least for a couple seconds. This is related to people's instinct to "hide their treasure" and not draw attention to something of value. *Continual staring at the board is a sign that nothing has caused a player to look away or think about the situation.* It's not super-reliable but it's reliable enough to encourage you to bet if you're at all on the fence in such a situation.

This would be a flop I would usually check back but seeing these players' behaviors I decide to bet $10 into the $17 pot. They both fold. If I did get a call, I am confident enough in these general patterns that I would probably be betting the turn also.

Hand #35: Checking after double-checking cards
$2-5 NLHE cash game

I make it $15 in late position with 7♦ 6♣. One player behind me calls and the big blind calls.

The flop is K♥ 8♥ 6♥.

The first player looks back at his cards for a second and says, "Check."

Again, double-checking cards from non-aggressors in such spots will make weak hands more likely. If he had flopped a flush or a set, it's unlikely he'd double-check his cards; he would generally not want to draw attention to himself. Also, verbal checks are small indicators of weakness: reliable, but not *very* reliable.

In a vacuum, I would check this flop, but knowing the first player is likely to be weak and knowing I'm mainly worried about the player behind me, it encourages me to bet this flop. I bet $25 into the $47 pot and they both fold.

Hand #36: Verbal statement when checking flop
$2-5 NLHE cash game

A good player raises to $15 on the button with Q♠ 6♠. The big blind calls, saying, "Let's see a flop."

The flop is A♦ 9♠ 6♥. The big blind checks, saying, "You win."

Most talking early in a hand from non-aggressors (checkers and callers) will be defensive in nature. Mainly, though, it will indicate that the player doesn't have a strong hand and isn't focused on the situation because, if they had a strong hand, they'd probably be focused and quiet.

In my book *Verbal Poker Tells*, I talk about how weak-hand statements from bettors will make weak hands unlikely. *For non-aggressors, though, any verbal statement weakens their range.* So even though this player is making a weak-hand statement, because he's a non-aggressor he's likely to be defensive and weak here.

In this case, the good player checks back with bottom pair. Considering how many bad cards are possible on the turn, and considering his opponent's behavior makes him likely to have a weak hand, I believe this makes a c-bet the best decision here.

Both players check it down. The big blind had K♥ 8♥.

Hand #37: Ostentatious check-behind from PFR
$2-5 NLHE cash game

A fairly tight player raises to $15 in late position. I call in the big blind with 9♠ 8♠.

The flop is Q♥ 7♠ 5♣. I check and the raiser checks

behind pretty quickly by waving his arms in an exaggerated, comical motion.

This ostentatious behavior makes strong hands (e.g., AQ, overpairs, sets) less likely than usual. Because he'd probably at least consider betting hands like 88-JJ, his pretty quick check also makes those hands less likely. Because he's a pretty tight player, his range is mostly AK and other strong Aces.

On a 5♥ turn, I bet $30 into the $32 pot and he folds.

If he were to call the turn, as some people will do when they play AK or a small pair this way, all of this information can make you more confident bluffing the river or, if you have a strong hand, it might influence you to size your bet smaller than usual on the river to try to get a call.

This player's very ostentatious checking motion is similar to more subtle checking motions. For example, you might see a player check back with an extended tapping of the table. The more unusual the behavior seems, the less likely it is that the player is checking back with a strong hand.

Hand #38: Subdued player raises suspicion

$1-2 NLHE cash game

There are two limps. I call in late position with A♥ 4♠. One player calls behind me.

It's five-way to a flop of 5♠ 5♣ 2♥. Three players check to me. Two of them sit staring at the flop, which makes it more likely they have weak hands. This encourages me to bet.

Then I notice the player behind me staring down at his lap, being very still compared to his usual demeanor.

Abnormally inconspicuous (non-ostentatious) behavior makes strong hands a bit more likely. It's not nearly as meaningful as ostentatious behavior, but it is slightly meaningful.

Another clue here: *in non-confrontational and small-stakes situations, a player acting strangely makes strong hands more likely.* If I noticed this same behavior in a raised heads-up pot, it probably wouldn't have much meaning, because players act more serious and restrained in those situations. But when it's a pretty boring, standard spot and a player is acting strangely subdued or inconspicuous, that should get your attention and be cause for concern.

Because this is a borderline spot for me to bet anyway, I opt to just check. The player in question bets $5 into $11 and everyone folds.

I don't think such a tell is reliable enough to get you to fold strong hands, but for borderline spots that could go either way, it can help you take a more cautious approach.

Hand #39: Eye flash weakens range
$5-10 NLHE cash game

In late position, I raise to $30 with J♠ T♠. The big blind, a decent player, calls.

The flop is K♠ 9♣ 6♣. My opponent is staring at the flop. When I turn my head and look over at him, his eyes go momentarily wide for a fraction of a second: this behavior is sometimes called an *eye flash*.

People will often perform an eye flash in response to someone looking at them. In social situations, people who are friendly with each other will perform eye flashes sometimes when passing by each other: it's a non-verbal way to acknowledge someone interacting with you. It's a way to respond in an interested way to something.

The eye flash in this situation can be understood as an ostentatious behavior from a non-aggressor, and ostentatious behaviors from non-aggressors make strong hands less likely.

My opponent is also staring at the flop, which also makes weakness more likely.

My opponent checks. I bet $50 into $65 and my opponent calls.

The turn is a second 6, making the board K♣ 9♣ 6♣ 6♦.

Encouraged by my opponent's behavior on the flop, I bet $130 into $165. He folds.

Again, it's entirely possible this player could have some decent hands, including some strong Kings. But the eye flash and the flop-stare make his strongest hands less likely, and his weaker range encourages me to bluff here. And I would also be betting the river if he called the turn.

Hand #40: Exclamation about board weakens range
$2-5 NLHE cash game

A good player makes it $15 in middle position. I call on the button with K♥ T♥. A tight player in the big blind calls.

The flop is Q♥ 7♥ 6♦. Immediately, the tight player exclaims, "Wow!" and then checks.

When players make immediate exclamations about the board, it's unlikely they've flopped very well. They might have flopped something decently strong but it just makes the strongest hands less likely. This is most useful on coordinated boards, like when there's a pair on the board, or three to a flush. But it's still generally useful as a small tell of weakness.

The pre-flop raiser checks, saying, "I never hit a flop." If this player were going to check a hand like a set, it's unlikely he'd say anything. (This is in keeping with the general pattern of early-hand talking usually being weakness.) What's most probable is he's just checking and giving up because he missed in a multi-way pot.

Both players' behaviors encourage me to bet. I bet $20 into $31. The tight player calls me. This is worrisome, but because I am confident the strongest hands are unlikely, I'm encouraged to continue bluffing. I think heart draws are possible as are hands like 99, TT, JJ, and 98s. AQ, KQ, and QJ are the hands I'm mainly worried about, as they're the only hands I think he'd continue with on the turn.

The turn is an Ace, giving me a gutshot straight draw. It's also a great card because it makes AQ less likely for him and it's become a scarier board for him if he has a Q. He checks and I bet $50 into $80. He folds, telling me that he had a heart draw.

If this player were to raise me on the flop or the turn, I would be folding. Even though his flop behavior makes weak hands more likely, it's just one piece of information. If he were to raise, I'm not confident enough in the behavior that I'd want to continue in the hand.

Hand #41: Caller statement weakens range

A $5-10 NLHE hand with Andrew Brokos

This next hand was played by Andrew Brokos. Andrew is a professional poker player and coach. He co-hosts a podcast and has a blog, both of which are available at ThinkingPoker.net. Andrew also makes instructional videos for Tournament Poker Edge and Red Chip Poker.

This hand was from a $5-$10 game with relatively deep stacks. The main Villain in the hand and I both had at least $3,000 on the table.

The UTG player limped, and I raised to $50 next to act with Q♣ Q♠. The main villain called UTG+2, and the BB and limper also called.

The flop came 9♥ 6♥ 6♣. As the dealer spread the flop, I watched BB and UTG to see their reactions to it. Given where everyone was seated relative to me, I could watch two of them, but not UTG+2. I didn't notice anything interesting from either of them, and they both checked to me.

I bet $125. UTG+2 called as he said, "You watched them. You weren't worried about me?"

This player's willingness to discuss the possibility of his having a strong hand made me think that he didn't have a strong hand. Generally a player who flopped a monster wouldn't want to call attention to that possibility. This gave me the confidence to continue value betting my hand with less fear of running into a big hand.

I bet $300 on the 3♣ turn and $700 on the 2♠ river. My opponent called all the way and mucked when I showed my hand.

Hand #42: Agitation of caller weakens range

$1-2 NLHE cash game

A loose player, who raises way too often pre-flop, raises to $6 UTG. There are four callers and I call in the BB with T♥ 5♥.

The flop is T♦ 6♥ 4♣. I check and the pre-flop raiser thinks.

As he considers, the player behind him looks at him agitatedly and impatiently. Again, this kind of ostentatious behavior from a waiting-to-act player makes it unlikely she has flopped well.

The pre-flop raiser bets $12 into $37. This small bet-sizing will usually be weak, both for this player specifically and for inexperienced players in general.

The player behind him, who seemed agitated, calls his bet.

Everyone else folds to me. I make it $36 and they both fold.

One of the factors here was that the flop caller was a fairly tight and predictable player. Taking into account her flop behavior, if she did call my flop raise, she probably had a better Ten and I thought it was likely she would fold to a large turn bet.

Without her behavior, I wouldn't have had any information about her range and would have just called the flop bet.

Hand #43: Question about bet amount before calling flop

$2-5 NLHE cash game

I raise to $25 in late position with 7♣ 6♣. The small blind calls. She's a bad player who plays passively and straightforwardly.

The flop is A♥ Q♥ 6♦. She checks and I bet $35 into $55.

She looks across the table at the bet questioningly and asks, "Thirty-five?" as if the bet size is a factor in whether she'll be calling or not. After an abnormally long pause of about ten seconds, she calls.

A seemingly minor clue, but in these early-hand situations I tend to think any somewhat ostentatious behavior makes very strong hands (sets, two-pair) less likely than normal.

For most loose-passive players, unusual pauses before a call make flush draws unlikely. Why is that? *For your average loose-passive player, they will almost always be calling with a flush draw in this spot, while at the same time hardly ever be raising.* The fact that they seem to be thinking about the situation makes a flush draw unlikely. And this is *not* true for aggressive players, because those players will usually at least consider raising with their draws.

Worth noting: such a pause here does *not* rule out super-strong hands, like a set. But often you will know strong hands are unlikely from the action; most players with strong hands will be betting or raising on the flop or turn, especially on boards with draws possible.

So with the two clues here (the question and the pause), I think weaker made hands are much more likely than a flush draw. It's possible she has an ace and will be calling a turn bet or more, but that's a chance I'm willing to take.

The turn is a 4♥, putting three hearts out. This is actually a great card for me if I think it's unlikely she has the flush draw. She checks and I bet $80 into $125. She folds T♣ T♥ face-up.

Deciding to base decisions on behavior in these kinds of spots will sometimes get you into gross situations. She might have had a hand like A♠ T♥ or A♠ J♥ and called the turn, and then I wouldn't really know where I was at and I'd have to decide whether to fire the river or give it up. And sometimes of course I'll be wrong and an opponent will show up with a strong hand and I'll be raised. But in the long-term, these little clues help me choose my bluffing spots better than I would be able to without them.

Hand #44: Immediate call from aggressive player
$2-5 NLHE cash game

A player puts out a $10 straddle UTG.

I have K♣ Q♠ in middle position. I don't notice the straddle and because of this I raise to only $20. The UTG straddler calls.

This player's range is obviously super-wide considering my min-raise. For a little history: this player is known for often being too-aggressive and is capable of doing some very weird things.

The flop is K♥ 5♣ 4♣. He checks. I bet $30 into $47 and he calls immediately.

Let's think about this immediate call. Immediate calls, in general, will indicate weak hands and weak draws. With strong hands on most boards, players will at least *consider* a raise for a second or two, even if they decide to slow-play. And if they flop a strong draw (for example, A♣ Q♣ on this flop) they will also usually consider a raise. This means most immediate calls on the flop and turn will be hands that a player considers obviously worth a call and also obviously not worth a raise; hands like top pair with a weak kicker, other one-pair hands, straight draws, and weak flush draws.

But in this situation this player's immediate call is even more meaningful than usual. This is because *this player is aggressive*. He looks for any opportunity to be aggressive. Even if he had a low flush draw, it's likely he'd *at least consider* a raise.

The turn is the T♠. I bet $70 into $107 and he again calls pretty quickly. This makes straight draws very unlikely; while he might snap call all sorts of straight draws on the flop, he'd be unlikely to do that for the larger turn bet.

The river is the K♣, giving me trips but also putting three to the flush out there. In a vacuum, without his behavior, I'd be checking here. But as it is, I think it's probable he has a one-pair hand.

I bet $100 into $247, purposefully sizing the bet on the lower side to try to get some weaker calls or induce bluffs. (A bigger bet or a check could easily be better choices than this.)

Immediately he puts out a raise to $300, with a kind of violent motion. I know this player is fully capable of bluffing here, especially taking into account my small river bet. I call and he says, "You're good" and mucks.

Now obviously I will be wrong sometimes here. If he *did* end up having a flush here, it would probably be a low one, which would help explain the immediate flop call.

Remember: part of my confidence in this read is based on this player being aggressive. For a more passive player, who won't automatically be thinking of raising with a flush draw, these ideas won't apply.

Hand #45: Snap-check from same aggressive player
$5-10 NLHE cash game

This hand features the same aggressive player from the last hand.

This player raises in early position to $30. I raise to $90 in middle position with A♣ A♥. He calls and we're heads-up.

The flop is J♥ 8♠ 4♥. He checks and I bet $110 into $195. He calls after around two seconds.

The turn is the 3♥, putting out three hearts. My opponent snap-checks to me.

This is a very similar situation: if this player had hit the flush, he would usually at least consider betting here. Again: part of what makes this so meaningful is that he's an aggressive player. He will usually want to get action on his strong hands and he is right to usually expect action. Even if he were going to check with the flush, it's likely he'd take a few seconds to decide that. Same if he'd flopped a set of Jacks; if he'd decided to slowplay them on the flop, it's likely he'd at least *consider* betting the turn.

Knowing this, the turn becomes an easier bet with hands you might otherwise be afraid to bet. In this case, though, I decided to check back. Part of my reasoning was that I had the A♥, so wasn't afraid of a heart falling and a heart might get me action I wouldn't otherwise get. Another reason was that I knew that my check might induce a lot of bluffs from him on the river. Another reason was that if he had hands like QQ or TT, he might fold those on the turn but call a bet on the river.

The river is the 3♠, pairing the board. Sure enough, my opponent fires out a pot-sized bet: $400 into $415. I don't really like this because I think it's bigger than he'd usually bet with a bluff, but if I think a flush is unlikely I have to call.

He shows J♠ T♠, for a pair of Jacks, and I'm good.

Hand #46: Thoughtful check from aggressive player contains clues
$5-10 NLHE cash game

This is another hand with that same aggressive player. He raises in middle position to $35 and gets three callers. The flop is 7♣ 5♦ 5♠. He's last to act and his opponents check to him. He plays with his chips as if indecisive about what to do. After several seconds, he checks.

When I saw this behavior, *I immediately thought he had trips or a full house.*

Here's why: if he had high cards that missed (AK, KQ, TJ, etc.) he'd just check immediately. He's a pretty experienced player and with three opponents, he's never going to be betting those hands. And he wouldn't Hollywood as if he had a decision in a multi-way pot; he's not that type of player.

If he had an overpair or a seven, he'd always be betting. I also think he'd usually be betting 66. And if he had any sort of straight draw (like 8-6, 6-4, maybe even 4-3) he'd almost always be betting.

So ruling all those hands out makes trip 5s or a full house very likely. Again, this read is only possible because this player is aggressive and will almost always be betting his decent hands and drawing hands.

If we think that with a flopped full house he'd often be quickly and inconspicuously checking back, then trips become even more likely than normal.

How might these thoughts affect your line in the hand?

- On the turn, if you had a very strong hand (strong trips, a full house, or a turned straight), you might make your bet-sizing larger than you normally would, being confident that you'd get action.

- With weaker hands, like overpairs, you could play the turn more cautiously: either checking and calling or checking and folding, depending on how confident you felt in your read.

This player ended up having 5♣ 4♠, for trips.

Hand #47: Quick bet and a possible reverse tell
$10K WSOP PLO tournament

In the 2017 WSOP $10K Pot Limit Omaha event, Tommy Le, the eventual winner, made a tough fold versus Scott Clements. The following is from the after-event interview, talking about that hand, with some slight edits:

A player limps on the button. I have Kings. I think double-suited. So I raise the pot. Scott had me covered a little bit. We were two of the biggest stacks. And I knew, when I raise pot, I saw Scott look at my stack, and I think he was trying to calculate if he could re-pot me back and get the majority of his chips in.

So he called. I wasn't really sure if had AA, but I knew he had a big hand. He didn't hesitate and he called pretty quick. So I knew it was one of those hands where the hand plays itself.

So he calls. Button folds. Flop comes A-K-9 rainbow. I make a standard bet. Like a third of the pot. And then, when I bet, he didn't really hesitate to raise. It took him a few seconds to make it 600, I think I bet 165, he made it 600, think it was. When he made it 600, I knew if he had AK he would probably call. Nines, same. Maybe raise. But I think he would have to think a little more.

So when he did an insta-raise I felt like he had maybe K-Q-J-T. But even that, he might call. Or like A-K, he could raise A-K, but my first instinct is he'd call. I have second set, so I should call there like 99% of the time. But then when I was tanking, I saw him breathe. He made this weird breathing gesture. He was breathing really hard. And we all know Scott's a pro, right? This is not his first rodeo. For him to do that, I felt like he was baiting me in. And the more I looked at him, the more he got nervous. So right there, I was like 99% sure he had Aces. So I laid the hand down.

Some thoughts: All of Tommy's points are interesting and likely to be generally valid, I think, especially when combined. Regarding the breathing: when a good player seems nervous or acts unusually when betting, it becomes more likely that it's a reverse tell. I often see experienced players giving away their level of relaxation in such ways.

I also think Tommy was primarily acting on fundamental reasons—that Scott was very unlikely to raise here without a very strong hand—and may have been over-emphasizing the tells in the excitement of the post-game interview.

We'll talk more about quick bets and unusual big-bet behavior later.

Hand #48: Break from stoic pose weakens range
$5-10 NLHE cash game

There's an early position limp. I raise to $30 in middle position with 9♠ 9♣.

A decent player on the button makes it $90. He's capable of three-betting with a wide range here because he knows that I have a fairly wide raising range and that I'll often be folding to a three-bet.

The third player calls and I do, too. The three-bettor and I have about $1,200 to start; the third player has about $800.

The flop is A♥ K♦ 3♠. The first player checks and I check. The three-bettor thinks for a few seconds and checks back.

Up until that moment, since his pre-flop raise, he'd had a very thoughtful, stoic demeanor. He was still and very focused. But after checking back, he kind of breaks out of his stoic pose and moves around, looking at me and the other player, licking his lips, and just having a looser demeanor in general.

When good players go from being stoic and focused to becoming more physically loose and unfocused, it will often indicate they've mostly given up on the hand. This isn't likely to happen in heads-up pots, because good players are more likely to look for any opportunity to win those pots. But in multi-way pots, when they decide they're "done with the hand" and likely not putting any more money in, sometimes they will let their guard down and seem obviously unfocused.

In this case, this player "breaking his pose" made it very unlikely he'd flopped a set, which was the main strong hand to worry about when he checks back on such a dry flop. Maybe he has air, maybe he has JJ or QQ, but the strongest hands have become less likely. Even hands like KQ or Kx suited have become less likely, because with a King he'd still have a reason to be mentally focused on the hand.

The turn is the 4♥. The first player checks. I bet $150

into $277. This is a bluff, because I think I can get the three-bettor to fold TT-QQ, and get the first player to fold similar hands and Kings. (And if I do happen to be ahead, there are many bad cards for me on the river.) Because I'm confident the pre-flop raiser isn't likely to be a threat, I'm more comfortable betting in this spot.

Both players fold.

Hand #49: Another break from a stoic pose

$2-5 NLHE cash game

A decent player raises to $20 in late position and I call in the big blind with A♠ 6♠.

The flop is 8♦ 7♥ 4♦. I check and he bets $25 into $42. I call. He's in a very stoic mode: very still and focused.

The turn is the Q♣. I check and, after a few seconds, he checks behind. As he checks, he breaks out of his stoic pose: he glances over at me and starts riffling his chips.

The river is the Q♠, pairing the board.

From a fundamental (non-behavior-related) perspective, his range at this point is mostly capped at medium pairs, around JJ-99, and 8s and 7s. His breaking out of his focused pose makes the strongest pairs less likely. With those hands, he'd have more of an incentive to stay focused and thoughtful.

Betting this river makes a lot of sense just fundamentally, but if you were on the fence at all, this player's stoic-pose-break makes it more likely than usual he'll be folding.

I bet $60 into the $92 pot and he folds.

Hand #50: Quick flop check from pre-flop raiser
$1-2 NLHE cash game

The UTG player raises to $5. A player calls on the button and I call in the SB with A♥ 5♥.

The flop is A♠ K♦ 5♣. I check and the pre-flop raiser checks immediately.

Immediate checks from pre-flop raisers will tend to define the player's hand as either:

- A good but not great hand (in this case, QQ and JJ would qualify)

- A very strong hand (in this case, AK, AA, or KK)

For your average amateur player, though, this pattern skews more towards very strong hands, and this is because these players will often at least consider the situation with their weaker hands for a moment.

Put another way: if this player had QQ, JJ, KQ, or weaker pairs, or if he had a weak Ace, it's probable he'd at least consider the situation for a second, even if he will usually end up checking. (One factor here is that many amateur players overvalue pocket pairs in general, so even with QQ on a flop of A-K-5, many players want to think about it for a few seconds.)

Experienced players are capable of quickly checking back decent-but-not-strong hands. For example, if this player were skilled, he would immediately recognize that he's not betting KQ or QQ here, whereas many amateur players with those hands will think for a few seconds.

When this player, who struck me as very inexperienced, checked second-to-act immediately, I was very wary.

The turn is a 9♥. I check again. The pre-flop raiser bets $17 into the $17 pot. The third player folds and I call.

I'm far from confident that he's flopped super-strong here, but one reason I check is that the board is quite dry. If I'm ahead, I will likely stay ahead, so there's not much risk in giving a free card. If the board were more draw-heavy, I'd have to be much more sure of my read than I was here.

The river is the T♦. I check and he checks back with A♣ K♠, top two pair. (Don't ask me why he checked.)

If he had made a decent-sized bet on the river, I'd be folding. For average players who raise pre, check the flop, and bet big on the turn and river, they'll usually be very strong. The immediacy of his flop check is just one extra hint that he's on the stronger side here.

Hand #51: Timing tells define range
$1-2 NLHE cash game

A strange, aggressive kid has been raising a lot pre-flop. Almost all of these raises have happened immediately, within a second.

In one hand, I notice that when action gets to him, he takes several seconds to raise to $10. In general, unusual pauses will make strong hands more likely. And for this specific player, it's likely to be quite meaningful. In the moment, I thought QQ+ was his most likely hand.

The raiser gets one caller behind him.

The flop is Q♠ T♣ 9♦.

The pre-flop raiser checks immediately first-to-act.

Again, an immediate check from the pre-flop raiser in such a spot is fairly rare. Considering he's aggressive, we'd expect him to be c-betting, or at least thinking about c-betting, with most of his range.

When I saw this player make an unusually long pause before raising pre-flop and then check immediately on this flop, I thought it was very probable that he'd flopped a set of Queens. It's not very common that you can feel confident putting a player on one specific hand, but when multiple tells are combined, it can make a read very precise. He did end up showing Q♥ Q♦.

What would be the practical benefits of noticing this if you were his opponent here?

- If you had flopped the straight, you might go for an overbet to try to get as much money in as possible.

- If you had flopped two-pair or a lower set, this behavior might encourage you to play the hand more cautiously than you otherwise would.

Hand #52: Another snap-check from PF raiser
$2-5 NLHE cash game

A tight player in early position raises to $15. I call in late position with 9♣ 8♣ and we're heads-up.

On a flop of T♣ 6♣ 5♦, he checks immediately. When an opponent checks immediately in a spot where I expect them to almost always be betting, I get suspicious. I check behind, as I think there's an above average chance he'll be check-raising me.

The turn is the Q♥. He bets $30 into $37 and I call.

The river is the J♣, giving me the flush. He makes an over-bet: $130 into $97.

This is kind of a gross spot. On the one hand, I can easily imagine him betting some weaker hands. I can imagine him betting a flopped set of Tens like this on the river, because my check-back of the flop makes me having the flush draw unlikely. While I can see him betting a random AK like this on the river if he's not afraid of me having a flush, I don't think he snap-checks the flop with his AK; I think he checks, yes, but just don't think he often snap-checks.

On the other hand, his immediate flop check makes me think A♣ K♣ is possible. The nut flush draw with AK is so strong that some players are capable of checking the flop quickly with it, like they might if they flopped a set. At the same time, that's not going to be very common.

I don't think there's anything else besides the hands I've mentioned that this particular player would have; he was not a bluffer and was not going to be betting weaker hands than a set.

I ended up calling and he had A♣ K♣: the nut flush. While the read and situation were a little too ambiguous for me to feel good folding the river, I think the flop check-back was a good decision that avoided bloating the pot.

I thought this was a good hand to include because it shows how a strong draw can feel like a strong hand to some players, which can result in them exhibiting strong-hand behavior. This kind of ambiguity is the major reason flop reads are generally hard to make.

Hand #53: Immediate flop call weakens range
$300 buy-in NLHE tournament

Early in this tournament, I raise to 350 with K♣ T♦ and get one caller in the BB.

The flop is A♥ 9♠ 6♥. He checks and I bet 400 into 775. He calls immediately.

The turn is a 3♣. He checks, I bet 900 into 1,575. He folds.

Without his immediate call on the flop, I probably would have just checked back the turn. *Immediate flop calls should usually encourage you to take a more aggressive line.*

Hand #54: Smiling and showing cards to neighbor weaken range

$1-2 NLHE cash game

There are two limps and I make it $14 with A♥ J♣. I get only one caller: a player behind me who is a loose, strange player. He smiles to himself as he calls; this makes it unlikely he has a strong hand.

The flop is 7♦ 2♦ 2♠. I bet $16 into $35.

He calls, showing his cards to his neighbor and smiling. His neighbor also looks amused. With this behavior, he's unlikely to have a 2 here; he'd tend to be focused and thoughtful with a 2, and less likely to show his neighbor.

His neighbor's behavior also makes it unlikely this player has a strong hand. If his neighbor saw that he had trips, for example, he would likely also be stoic and thoughtful. *He'd instinctually be concerned about potentially giving away the strength of his neighbor's hand, and that would make him more cagey and stoic.*

I think this player's most probable hand is a weak 7 or else an underpair to the 7. A hand like 33 would easily account for the amusement of both players.

I think it's also possible, though unlikely, that he has AK. You will sometimes see a player show AK to a neighbor in a way that implies, "This damn hand never hits for me."

The turn is the K♣, still no draw. The pot is $67.

My opponent bets $20 out of turn behind me, before I've acted. I think this is probably just a little tricky ploy to slow me down. Considering his most likely range, it's unlikely the King helped him. If he did have AK, though, it's unlikely he'd bet out-of-turn. With a hand that strong, I think he'd be more stoic and cagey. Also, if he had AK, he'd probably bet more.

The house rules are that if I bet, changing the action, he can take his bet back. But if I check, his action stays the same, and his bet remains. I decide to check and have him bet the $20. Then I check-raise to $55.

He calls after a few seconds, with only $65 behind. I had thought a fold was probable, so this was not a good result, but I feel committed to shove on the river no matter what comes.

The river is an offsuit Q. The board is 7-2-2-K-Q. I bet his remaining $65 and he folds. Whatever he had, he played it strangely, but if I had to guess, I'd say it was probably 3-3 or 4-4.

Although it worked out well here, my turn raise was small and bad in hindsight. I think it would have been better to either lead out normally (not let him bet the $20) or to shove after his $20 turn bet. The point, though, is that his small clues of weakness and lack of focus encouraged me to take a more aggressive line.

Hand #55: Ostentatious placement of chips from flop caller

$2-5 NLHE cash game

There is a $10 UTG straddle. The small blind calls and I raise to $50 with A♥ A♣ in the big blind. Both players call.

The flop is T♣ 9♦ 5♦. I bet $100 into $150, the player behind me calls quickly. He calls by putting a large chip stack next to my bet, using the height of my bet stack to measure his bet. He only has $250 behind.

This is another example of an ostentatious, attention-grabbing behavior from a non-aggressor that you see somewhat often. This behavior makes me confident that this player didn't flop a set or two-pair.

Also, the quick call is probably meaningful. Considering his short stack, I think if he had a flush draw or an open-ended straight draw here, he'd almost always consider shoving. So not only does his combined behavior make strong hands unlikely, it also makes draws less likely.

The small blind folds so it's heads-up. The turn is the 7♦, putting three diamonds out. Without his immediate flop call, I'd be checking to him, possibly giving him a free draw if he were to check behind.

But because a flush is unlikely for him, I bet his remaining $250 into the $350 pot. I think he's capable of calling with a ten or a flush draw.

He calls and turns over T♥ 7♥: he'd hit two-pair on the turn.

Hand #56: An immediate call as a false tell
2007 WSOP Main Event

It's folded around to the blinds. The small blind calls. Hevad Khan, a professional player, checks with K♦ 8♣ in the big blind.

The flop is A♦ T♣ 8♥. Both players check.

The turn comes the 8♠, giving Khan trips.

The SB bets and Khan snap-calls.

Recounting this in an interview later, Khan said, "I super-fast call to make it look like I'm on a draw, because a quick call usually implies weakness."

The more experienced an opponent is, the less you can trust the common reads. Experienced players will know the generally understood meanings and so are more likely to reverse those meanings.

Having said that, false tells are pretty rare, even from experienced players. Most experienced players strive for stoic unreadability. *Most players just want to avoid giving off tells; they don't want to get into complex mind games with opponents.*

If you do notice an opponent who seems to purposefully reverse a behavior, this can be valuable information. For example, if you saw a player snap-call the turn with trips, it's easy to remember that that player is capable of being tricky, and you'll want to a) be less likely to act on his behavior, and b) observe him to see if his reverse-tells are themselves reliable tells. *A reverse tell, if it's done often enough, is just a tell.*

Most attempts at false tells, even from experienced players, will make use of commonly understood tells. (One example: you'll sometimes see an experienced player, when bluffing, call the clock on his opponent, in an attempt to "level" that opponent; this is because calling the clock on an opponent is a commonly understood, general tell of relaxation and a strong hand.) If you see an experienced player do something that is a widely understood indicator of weakness, you should consider the possibility that they're doing it purposefully.

Hand #57: Defensive chip handling from caller
$1-2 NLHE cash game

A tight player limps early. I make it $12 with K♥ Q♠ on the button. The big blind and the tight limper call.

The flop is 9♣ 4♣ 3♣. Both opponents check and I bet $22 into $37. Only the tight player calls me.

The turn is the Q♦, giving me top pair. My opponent touches his chips, as if thinking about betting. He checks and looks at me intently.

A waiting-to-act player or non-aggressor who handles chips in an interested way will usually be weak. I call this *defensive chip handling* or, more generally, because chips aren't always involved, *defensive hand movements*.

These kinds of behaviors make the strongest hands less likely. If this player had flopped a flush, he'd not want to put up an obstacle to my bet. These behaviors can be very obvious, especially at low-stakes games. More commonly, they are fairly subtle, with a player just gently touching his stack or barely reaching towards his chips.

I bet $40 into $81 and he calls. With his call, I'm thinking it's probable he has a hand like A9 or T9 with a club or TT with a club.

The river is the 5♣, putting four clubs out. Again, this player is stroking his chips and staring at me in what I think is a defensive way. He checks. I do think it's likely he has a club but with his behavior it's not likely to be the A♣. I bet $100 into $161.

After a few seconds of deliberation, he folds.

Hand #58: Defensive behavior encourages slowplay

$1,000 buy-in NLHE tournament

Here's a situation where defensive chip handling encouraged me *not* to bet a strong hand.

It's fairly early in this tournament. The blinds are 400-800. There's one limp UTG+1. I make it 2100 with A♣ K♦. Only the button calls.

The flop is K♥ 4♠ 2♦.

My opponent, an older guy who has played very badly and tightly so far, is making all kinds of obvious, textbook defensive chip handling moves. He's grabbing his chips in one hand, as if ready to call me. He's staring at me steadily, which also makes it likely he's in defensive mode.

I don't see him having KQ here; I don't think he would be that defensive. Based on his style of play, I don't think he called with a weaker King. So he's probably got a hand like 99 or 88, something like that, and I can easily see him folding this on the flop or if not the flop, then the turn. I don't see myself making much money here.

But if I slowplay, maybe there's a chance he takes the lead in the hand. So I check, but he checks behind.

The turn is another 4. I debate betting again, but I decide to check again for the same reasons. I think there's a good chance he bets whatever he has, even if it's AQ. I check, but he checks again.

The river is a third 4. I bet 2,000 into 5,400. He folds immediately.

I'm not sure about my line in this hand; I think betting the flop would have been a fine thing to do to get at least one call from an underpair. Also, on the river, it might have been better to make an even smaller bet to try to get a light call.

But the main point is that, considering this player's tightness, his likely range, and the board, his defensive chip handling made it less likely he was going to give me significant action. If he'd been a looser opponent, I would have played it more straightforwardly, even with the defensive chip handling, as there'd be more of a chance I'd get paid.

Hand #59: Agitated reaction to impending call
$1-2 NLHE cash game

I limp under-the-gun with A♦ J♦. Six players see a flop of A♠ 5♣ 3♦.

The big blind bets $5 into $12. I make it $20. A player right behind me says, "All in," for $110. Everyone folds to me.

From what I know of this player, he's usually going to have at least a strong Ace. He's tight and passive: the kind of player who's fully capable of limping AQ and AK and then shoving with it here. I think his range here is around AT+, and weighted a bit more to AQ than AT.

I don't think he'd often play two-pair or a set this way; I think he'd probably make a smaller raise.

I ask him, "What you got?"

He quickly and agitatedly says, "Two cards." This seems relaxed and slightly goading, and would generally make a weak hand a little less likely. At the same time, I think he will usually have an Ace here, so I don't think there's much additional information in the response.

As I consider, I reach for my chips, as I might do if I was getting ready to call. At the same time, in reaction, my opponent touches his chips. He also starts shuffling his cards agitatedly.

This makes up my mind and I call. He has A♥ T♦.

When a player with a strong hand thinks you're calling, he'll generally not put up an obstacle to you making the call. In this case, if this player had AK or AQ, he'd likely know that he was ahead from my uncertainty, and if he saw me assembling chips for a call, he'd probably just let me follow through. *Generally, anything out-of-the-ordinary a player does when he thinks you're going to call, whether it's physical movement or talking, will make weak hands more likely.*

This is of limited reliability. This is especially true considering this player was pretty timid to begin with, and thus more likely to be nervous or agitated with a wide range of hands. I wouldn't have been terribly surprised if he had a stronger hand here. But the point is that it was fundamentally a borderline spot and therefore a good spot to use some behavioral information, even if that information was far from 100% reliable.

This general concept works the same for bettors who do something in response to an opponent who's getting ready to fold. For example: if I'd instead acted like I was ready to fold, and this player started doing something unusual, no matter what it was, it becomes more likely he has a strong hand and is trying to make a last-ditch effort to get me to reconsider and make the call.

Hand #60: Defensive chip handling from waiting-to-act player

$20-40 Limit Hold'em cash game

This is a $10-20 limit Hold'em kill pot, so it's $20-40. The "killer" is in the big blind; he puts up $20 instead of $10.

I have 2♣ 2♦ in early position. There are only 8 players at the table and I notice two players behind me folding or leaving the table. I raise. I get two callers behind me.

The flop is 9♣ 8♦ 4♠.

As I think for a moment, the player two behind me acts defensively: he grabs his chips and assembles them out in front of his stack, as if ready to call. I've played a lot with this player and he's very predictable. He often acts in agitated ways like this, and these behaviors are almost always weak, trying to discourage action.

This encourages me to bet. The first player folds and the defensive player calls.

The turn is the 9♦, putting two diamonds out.

The player is still holding his chips out, as if ready to call. This is not meaningful here, though. *Once a player takes a pose, it doesn't mean much when that pose is just "carried over" from the previous round.* He could have hit his card, he might have missed: there's not any new information. All we really know is that he started doing it on the flop, so he was probably weak then.

I bet again and this time he raises me immediately.

I don't think he has a lone 9 in his hand; he called a raise cold, pre-flop. Also, his defensive flop behavior is highly correlated to weak hands. At the same time, he's not an aggressive player, and usually when he raises, he does have a strong hand. I end up folding without giving it as much thought as I should have.

After I fold, he shows the hand that I quickly realize is the only hand that makes sense with all the information available: A♦ K♦. He cold-called a raise pre-flop, acted defensively as he called on the flop, and then the turn encouraged him to raise.

His hand actually becomes more transparent with the turn raise; more so than a call could ever make it. In other words: there are plenty of made hands he could have *called* me with on the turn, but very few that a straightforward, non-aggressive player would *raise* me with there. With his flop defensiveness and call, there is one hand that makes the most sense: A♦ K♦.

This hand reinforces the importance of taking behavior into account alongside fundamental hand reading and strategy. It also shows the importance of taking your time to think things through.

Hand #61: Casual call of big bet makes strong hand likely

$2-5 NLHE cash game

The game is short-handed, with 7 players. In the hijack, I raise to $20 with 5♥ 4♥. I get three callers: one behind me and two in the blinds.

The flop is 5♦ 4♣ 3♦.

Two players check and I bet $50 into $80. The player right behind me only has $250 and he shoves. Based on his playing style, his range is quite wide on this board, including many draws and pair-with-a-straight-draw type hands.

Action is on the player in the big blind. He and I both have around $600 remaining. He is a thinking player and he is *not* loose-passive. He fairly quickly and casually calls the $250. There is no real thought apparent; it's just very casual, almost as if he's thinking about something else entirely.

Casual calls from decent players, when there is significant action still possible, should make your alarm bells go off. With medium-strength hands and draws, most players will want to give the situation some thought, especially with another player behind them. They may not want to make their thoughtfulness very obvious, but there will usually be at least a few seconds pause, maybe some studying of the bettor or the player behind them, maybe some slight furrowing of the brow, or signs of alertness. When I saw this player make this call fairly quickly, with no signs of thoughtfulness, I immediately thought he had flopped either a set or a straight and was trying to get me in the pot.

This was a tough one, as I hadn't played that much with this player in the recent past and wasn't very confident in my read. I did eventually fold and the "casual caller" showed 7♣ 6♦ for the flopped straight.

Note that quick, casual calls indicating a strong hand are different from other, more standard immediate calls, which usually indicate a weak hand. Two differences:

- The casual calls with a strong hand are for a lot of money (whereas quick calls indicating weak hands are usually made early in a hand, for fairly small amounts).

- With casual calls with s
  potential action after the c
  with weak hands are usually d
  player, who has less to think abou

Hand #62: Another casual call

$2-5 NLHE cash game

I raise to $15 UTG+1 with 9♣ 8♣ and get three ca
The flop is J♣ J♥ T♣. We all check.

The turn is the 2♥, putting out two hearts. The small
blind checks and the big blind, a too-aggressive, too-loose
player, bets $20 into $60. I think this player would almost
always be betting bigger with trips on such a draw-heavy
board. With that in mind, I raise to $65.

A player folds. The button calls quickly and casually.

This is a similar spot as the last hand. What hand would
this player check back the flop with but be willing to make
a quick, casual call with on the turn? In the moment, I
thought there was a very good chance this player flopped
the boat with JT or JJ.

This player was quite tight and cautious. If he had a
weak Jack, he probably would have bet the flop. With a
strong Jack, he'd probably want to think a little bit before
deciding whether to call or raise the turn bet. If he had
a flush or straight draw, he would also likely think a bit
before calling the turn raise on a paired board.

The first bettor, in the big blind, calls the raise.

The river is the 7♣, giving me the straight flush. The
board is J♣ J♥ T♣ 2♥ 7♣.

The first player checks. The third player behind me has

rong hands, there is still
all (whereas quick calls
one by the last-to-act
t).

lers.

use, I'm going to
But I'd also like
who I think it's
g that the third
might seem a
t that this spe-
to call in that

to $270. The
alls. I raise to
ne, talking to
confident he
ong hand, so I think he may just be acting a bit to try to get the third player to call. He eventually calls and the third player folds.

This player had 2♣ 2♦, for the turned boat. His worried behavior on the river had been genuine. But on the turn, his casual call of the raise made a very strong hand likely.

Hand #63: Stack-studying by pre-flop raiser weakens range

$5-10 NLHE cash game

I raise in late position to $30 with 7♣ 7♥. A loose-passive player three-bets to $110 from the SB. I call. I have $1,400 and he has me covered.

The flop is A♥ Q♠ 3♦. Immediately my opponent starts to survey my stack in a very ostentatious way, lowering his head and moving around so he can see my chips better. Early in a hand like this, this kind of ostentatious behavior will make strong hands unlikely. If this player had flopped a set, it's likely he'd be more cagey and focused, at least for a little while.

And because checking out someone's stack can be seen as potentially intimidating, he probably wouldn't want to do that with a strong hand; he wouldn't want to scare me off. And this is mainly a factor of the pot being small; early in a hand, players with strong hands will generally be focused on getting action, and won't want to put up any obstacles to action. If this player had flopped a set, for example, and was genuinely curious about my stack size, he'd probably try to inconspicuously survey my stack, or else he'd wait until a little bit later in the hand, perhaps between streets, to try to get that information.

This behavior in this situation would probably mainly make two-pair and sets unlikely; I could imagine him doing such a thing with AK and weaker. Top pair is decently strong but it's also weak enough that most players don't mind too much if they don't get action.

But he doesn't bet; he checks. This behavior becomes even *more* meaningful for a non-aggressor. Because if he were going to slowplay, he'd especially not want to draw attention to himself and potentially spook me out of betting. Like most unusual behaviors from a non-aggressor, this will make weak hands more likely. In this situation and knowing this player's style of play, I think KK and JJ are very likely.

I bet $150 into $230. He thinks for a while and folds. If he had called, I would have thought KK was very probable and I would have also bet the turn.

Hand #64: Another surveying of opponent's stack
$5,000 buy-in NLHE tournament

This is a hand included in my poker tells video series (ReadingPokerTells.video). In this hand, a player raises pre-flop and professional player Victor Ramdin three-bets with A♦ K♣.

The flop is 7♥ 4♠ 3♠. Victor is first-to-act and immediately moves his head around, trying to check out his opponent's chip stack in an obvious, ostentatious way. Then he checks.

Again, just as in the last hand, this behavior makes it unlikely Victor has a strong hand. In this case, it means it's less likely he's flopped a set or has decided to play a high pair in a tricky way.

Hand #65: Aggressive donk-bet weakens range
$2-5 NLHE cash game

I raise to $20 in late position with A♣ 8♦. One player calls me in the BB; she's a pretty tight player but capable of the occasional unusual or aggressive play.

The flop is Q♦ Q♠ 9♣. She donk-bets $15 into the $40 pot. She fires it towards me aggressively.

Ostentatious behaviors early in a hand, when the pot is small, will make weak hands more likely. When the pot is small most players with strong hands will be thinking more about how to best play their hand to make the most money, and not want to scare an opponent away. This makes their behavior generally more gentle.

 As explained earlier, this bettor behavior becomes less reliable the later in the hand it is. This is because on later streets:

- There's less to actually think about on later streets.
- The bigger the pot gets, the less concerned a strong-hand bettor is about potentially scaring off an opponent, which makes it more possible they would do aggressive or ostentatious things.

But for small-pot, early-hand situations, it's fairly reliable.

Little clues like this are most useful on scary, have-it-or-you-don't boards (examples: paired boards, four-flush boards), where a bettor will usually either have a very strong hand or a hand with which they feel quite vulnerable. In this hand, I thought it was unlikely this player would act in an aggressive, forceful way if she had trip Qs.

The small bet-sizing is also a clue that she is probably weak. Most small donk-bets, as they're called, will be done with weak hands, to test the waters.

I min-raise her $15 bet to $30.

I don't think the min-raise here is a good strategy in general, but I think it's an okay strategy versus a predictable, passive opponent. I think her reaction to the raise could easily tell me a lot about her hand. For example: if she reraises me, I feel fine folding. Another example: if she calls fairly quickly, it's become less likely she has a Queen. It also costs me less than a larger raise if I continue to bluff and she doesn't fold.

In this case, she actually folds to the min-raise. If she had called, I would almost always be bluffing on the turn.

Hand #66: Quick, forceful bet weakens range
$2-5 NLHE cash game

Two players limp and we are 4-way to the flop. I have J♦ T♥ in the BB.

The flop is 6♠ 6♣ 2♠.

The SB and I both check and the early-position player, a very tight player, bets $20 into $20 quickly and forcefully.

In a vacuum, without behavior, this player is fully capable of having AA and KK; he is known for limping those hands early and trying to reraise. But his ostentatious, aggressive behavior makes strong hands less likely. In this case, I think it's unlikely he has AA, KK, or a 6.

The other two players fold and I call, intending to take the pot away later in the hand. (I think a raise is better here, though.)

The turn is a 9♠, putting three spades out.

I check. He checks behind, saying, "Oh, really?"

Small verbal statements from non-aggressors make weak hands more likely. In the off-chance he would play a 6, 22, or 99 like this, this verbal behavior makes those hands much less likely.

The river is the Q♥, making the board: 6♠ 6♣ 2♠ 9♠ Q♥.

I bet $40 into $60 and he folds, showing 4♣ 4♠.

Chris Moneymaker gets a read

Chris Moneymaker is a professional poker player and the winner of the 2003 WSOP Main Event. In the 2011 PokerStars Caribbean Adventure (PCA) tournament, Moneymaker got a read on an opponent, Chris Oliver.

In the footage from that event, Moneymaker tells a friend on the rail, "I think I've got something on Chris [Oliver]. I think he has a little bit of a tell... I know when he's going to play a hand, I think. He looks at his cards out of turn, and I think I've picked up on when he's going to play and when he's not going to play."

In the few hands they showed between these two players, it did seem to be true that Moneymaker had some sort of reliable read on Oliver, whatever it was. Oliver was extremely aggressive, putting Moneymaker to some tough decisions, and Moneymaker made the right decisions in the majority of hands they showed. Moneymaker ended up getting 11th place out of 1,560 players.

Below are two hands that serve as supporting evidence for Moneymaker's read:

Hand #1:

Moneymaker raises to 90K with 9♠ 9♥, Oliver three-bets to 200K with 6♥ 2♥, and Moneymaker calls.

On a flop of K♦ J♣ 8♠, Moneymaker checks and calls.

On a turn of T♠, Moneymaker checks. Oliver bets 509K into 958K. Moneymaker shoves for 1.66M.

Oliver folds.

Hand #2:

Oliver raises to 88K with 7♥ 5♥. A player calls in the SB with A♦ 3♦. Chris Moneymaker calls in the BB with Q♦ J♠.

The flop is J♣ 7♦ 5♠, giving Oliver two-pair. The SB checks, Moneymaker checks, and Oliver bets 135K.

Moneymaker calls.

The turn is the 6♠. Moneymaker checks. Oliver bets 260K. Moneymaker questions Oliver for a while, and eventually folds top pair.

In 2016, PokerListings.com interviewed Moneymaker about his read in that game, and he said the following:

"[Oliver] was in almost every single hand. I understood quickly that this was the guy I had to pay attention to. Right away I picked something up when he looked at his cards out of turn. I saw his demeanor change depending on the action in front of him. His demeanor also changed when the flop came out, depending on if he had hit something... These changes were all very subtle. The way he moved his hand when he put the chips in, breathing patterns; it was like the aura around him would vary."

Moneymaker makes a good point here; *when you are deciding where to concentrate your efforts of observation, the looseness of opponents should be a factor in your decision.* For one thing: if a loose, aggressive player does have some sort of behavioral pattern, there'll be a large sample size of hands for you to study. For another reason: you're more likely to be in pots with these types of players.

I studied the footage of that event, looking for what Moneymaker might have noticed. While it was a small sample size, I noticed that Oliver seemed to be much more agitated and animated when betting his weak hands. He looked around a lot, he bet quickly, he threw his chips out rather recklessly.

In the hand where he had 7-5 and flopped two pair, he was very subdued: much more calm and focused.

I asked Moneymaker if what he'd picked up on was a correlation between Oliver moving around a lot and him having a weak hand. Moneymaker confirmed this, saying:

"Yes, that was what I was alluding to in the interview when I talked about his betting style and 'aura'. It's like he was aggravated when he had a bad hand. It was the same post-flop and pre-flop. The pre-flop agitation is something I look for, especially when someone is card dead and more likely to be frustrated."

This is a common pattern that it pays to look for. It's a player-specific pattern, and if you spot it, it can be very valuable. And as Moneymaker points out, *the more active an opponent is, the more you get to study them and possibly correlate something.*

In that same 2016 interview, Moneymaker continued talking about poker tells:

Another example: card protectors. Many players like to use them and in a tournament they almost subconsciously will use their card protectors every single hand. But three hours later they've gotten lazy, and they're not using it anymore, and when they look at their cards out of turn you can see they want to fold before it even gets to them.

Some players move their cards two inches closer to them, some move them a little further away. All these are hints that I'm making mental notes of to use for future reference.

In today's game, many players think that tells are overrated; they don't believe in them anymore. Especially people who come from online poker; they think tells are overrated and that you can't really get any good information anymore. I disagree. Sometimes I'm wrong and I look like an idiot. Most of the time it leads to more chips.

Moneymaker makes good points about small pre-flop indicators. Those are some of the most useful things to concentrate on. This is especially true in tournaments, because players will try to have certain routines, and when they deviate from those routines there can be valuable information present.

Hand #67: Scared players may not fit common patterns
$2-5 NLHE cash game

A player raises to $20 and three players see a flop of J♥ T♥ 9♠. The pre-flop raiser bets $30 and another player snap-shoves for $300. She pushes her chips in with a lot of forward force.

The other players fold and the all-in player shows Q♦ 8♦ for the straight. She explains, "I just wanted to end it there."

While it's generally true that players with big hands, when the pot is small, behave in gentler, inconspicuous ways, it becomes less true for players who are playing in a tight, scared way. For players who just want to "end it" when they have a strong hand, it becomes more likely they'll act in forceful, aggressive ways that could possibly scare off opponents, which more experienced players generally avoid doing with strong hands.

For these players you have to give their bets more respect and recognize that it's easily possible for them to have the nuts even if they're doing things that seem like they don't want action, like snap-shoving or verbally discouraging action.

A little while later, this hand happens:

Six players call a $25 raise. The flop is T♥ 6♣ 4♥. The same player snap-shoves $400 into a $150 pot. She's called and she has 6♦ 6♠. Most players wouldn't be snap-shoving with a dominating hand here, but as we've seen, she's quite happy taking down pots when she can.

Hand #68: Early reach-for-chips weakens range
$1-2 NLHE cash game

There are two limpers and I limp on the button with 5♣ 4♣. It's 5-way to a flop of J♥ J♠ 3♣.

It's checked around to the guy in front of me, a tighter, cautious older guy. Before action gets to him, I see him reaching for chips. He bets $5 into $10.

I think it's very unlikely he has a Jack; most people with trips here wouldn't be reaching for chips before it's their turn. I think it's probable he has a hand like 77.

I call behind him. A small factor in me doing this is that I have three to the straight flush. If this were heads-up or three-way, I would call him with any two cards, as a pure float. But in this case, with three other players in the hand, I'm aware one of them might have a strong hand so I want a little potential to go with the float. If I didn't have some small possibility of a strong hand, I'd just fold. But mainly I'm calling because I'm quite sure the bettor is weak.

Another player calls. He's a very loose player, so I'm not concerned yet with his call. He's also smiling to himself as he calls; this also makes it less likely he has a strong hand.

The turn is another 3, putting two-pair on the board. Both players check in front of me. They both look towards me while I think. This makes me feel better about the situation; staring from players who are waiting for you to act will generally indicate defensiveness.

I bet $12 into $25. The loose guy folds and the flop bettor, the tight guy, calls. I still put him on a hand like 77.

The river comes and the board is J♥ J♠ 3♣ 3♦ 8♠. The tight guy checks and is staring at me hard. Not that it really matters, as I'm committed to betting at this point.

I bet $40 into $49. I purposefully size it a bit large; knowing what I know about him, he's unlikely to call a big bet.

He shows 4♠ 4♥ and folds.

Hand #69: Another early reach-for-chips
$5-10 NLHE cash game

I limp UTG with 3♦ 3♥. There's no raise and it's 5-way to a flop of K♦ K♠ 6♣.

I'm third to act and I bet $25 into $50. Before I reach for chips to bet, I see the player behind me reaching for chips prematurely as if ready to bet. This makes me confident he doesn't have a King.

He makes it $70. Everyone else folds. I reraise to $170 and he folds.

I think it's likely he had a hand like 88 or 99.

Hand #70: Check after pre-loading chips
$2-5 NLHE cash game

Doug Hull has been playing poker since 2001. He's the author of *Poker Plays You Can Use* and *Poker Work Book for*

Math Geeks, and the co-founder of the poker training site RedChipPoker.com. Here's a hand he played where tells came into play:

The game is $2-5 NLHE. The villain is an older man. He was constantly acting out-of-turn and massively telegraphing his actions before the action got to him. Very reliable in a truthful, straightforward way. It mostly hadn't mattered so far because we were on opposite sides of the table from each other.

Now to the hand.

The villain limps. I raise to $15 on the button with T♣ T♠. The villain is the only caller.

Flop is K♥ 8♠ 3♣. The villain checks.

A c-bet here with TT is fine, but I check back. I expect this Villain to be very straightforward on the turn. He will bet the King if he has it, check if he does not. I can then bet my TT on the turn when checked to.

After I check back and the dealer starts to deal the turn, the villain starts to pre-load his chips for a bet. He has the King. I'm confident of that and I'm done with the hand.

But then the turn comes out: an off-suit A♦.

Villain now looks at the Ace. After a pause, he awkwardly checks; this is the first time he has pre-loaded a bet and then not followed up with a bet. I think this has an obvious surface-level meaning: he has a King and hated the Ace.

My plan now is to bet and barrel unless another King comes on the river.

I bet $25 into about $30. The villain calls.

The river brings an Ace; the board is K♥ 8♠ 3♣ A♦ A♣. The villain donk-bets $30 into $85. This looks like what I call the "name your own price" type of blocking bet. I raise to $130 and he quickly folds.

Had this player not done the pre-load before the turn and then the stutter-step when checking, we likely check down and he wins $30. Instead he lost $55 more and doesn't get to showdown with the winning hand.

Hand #71: Check-in-the-dark helps define range
$2-5 NLHE cash game

There's one limp. I raise in late position to $20 with K♣ 9♣ and get two callers.

The flop is Q♦ 9♠ 3♦. Both players check and I bet $40 into $65. The big blind calls and the limper folds. The BB is a decent though mostly straightforward player, a bit too tight to be very dangerous.

The turn is the A♠. He checks and I bet $115 into $145. I think he'll fold a good amount of better hands. He calls.

Before the river comes, my opponent checks dark.

What does this tell us?

For one thing, it makes it unlikely that he has either of the flush draws. It's rare for anyone to check dark first-to-act with any sort of decent draw. People who are drawing want to bet if they hit their hand, or at least *consider* betting even if they end up checking.

Another factor: I've played with this player and consider him somewhat decent. From my experience, I don't think he'd check dark like this unless he had something decently strong that he usually intends to call the river with. Checking dark seems so obviously weak and I think he'd be aware of this, so I don't think he'd check dark here with very vulnerable hands like a lone Queen or a hand like TT.

I start wondering if he has maybe A-9 for two pair. Or maybe Q-9.

The river board is Q♦ 9♠ 3♦ A♠ 5♦. My opponent has already checked. Encouraged by knowing he is very unlikely to have diamonds, and also by knowing he's not a player who doesn't like to make big calls, I bet $300 into $375. After a long deliberation, he calls. He has Q-9.

Based on my read of this player's range, I would not have bluffed the river if the third diamond hadn't arrived. I wouldn't have bluffed a spade as I believed my opponent was committed to calling most rivers and the runner-runner draw wouldn't be very scary to him.

Hand #72: Immediate bet polarizes, weakens range
2013 European Poker Tour €10K buy-in NLHE tournament

Jason Lavallee min-raises to 60,000 from middle position and Carla Sabini calls on the button. The BB also calls.

The flop is 9♦ 8♥ 3♠ and Lavallee c-bets for 78K. Sabini calls.

The turn is the 3♥. Lavallee checks and Sabini quickly bets 100K. Lavallee calls.

The river is the K♠. Lavallee checks and Sabini again quickly bets 160K , around a third of the pot.

Lavallee makes the call with Q♣ J♣, beating Sabini's Q♦ T♦.

Lavallee talked afterward in a PokerNews.com interview with Kristy Arnett about how his opponent's bet-timing was a factor in his call:

I ended up checking [the turn] and she made a pretty small bet but really fast. Which against non-experienced players, usually, one of their biggest leaks is not value-betting light enough and just in general playing too polarized, where they'll bet their really big hands or their absolute air, but they won't really know what to do with the middle part of their range. Like if she shows up on the turn with like 87 suited, which is middle pair, I wouldn't expect her to bet really quickly; she would consider what to do with that hand.

And usually in tournaments, they'll opt even more for pot-control lines, which means not betting and being put to a tough decision, and instead try to steer the hand toward showdown. So when she bet really quickly it was an interesting decision because, I didn't think she had total air, but I wasn't sure what she would end up doing with like a 9, an 8, or like pocket 6s type of hand, and I didn't think that she would bet it that quickly.

So, I thought about raising, but I didn't see what raising would accomplish, because the stuff that I actually end up beating, stuff like 6-7 suited, JT, and QT, I already beat with my specific hand. So I decided to call instead, which is very non-conventional; it's one of those things that you, in the moment, you feel or you don't. There's something to be said about instinctual play; it's definitely not a standard line that I take all the time.

And the river brought an off-suit King. And I checked and she bet really fast again.

Lavallee explains in a clear way how quick bets can polarize a player's hand range. This is probably the most important and reliable aspect of quick bets: *they make medium-strength hands unlikely because most players need to consider what to do with medium-strength hands*, whereas with clearly strong and clearly bluff-worthy hands there is less thought required.

Besides this basic reason, we also have the fact that bluffers often wish to appear confident, which leads to them betting quickly. Conversely, players with very strong hands can have a motivation to appear uncertain, which can lead to them physically or verbally "hemming and hawing" (to quote Phil Hellmuth) before betting. For these reasons, quick bets will make it a bit more likely than usual that a bet is a bluff. But this is not a big factor; you should always remember that overall, most significant bets will be value-bets and not bluffs.

I wanted to include Lavallee's exact words because it's not often that experienced high-stakes players talk about how opponent behavior can influence their decisions. Many serious players don't like to talk about such things because they feel it reduces their edge—and they're probably right.

Hand #73: Tilt of head strengthens bettor's range
$2-5 Crazy Pineapple cash game

This hand was sent to me by Drew Epstein, a former full-time pro poker player:

> The villain and I are friends with occasional bluffy, aggressive dynamics, although we have a ton of respect for each other's game. We are about $1,000 effective stacks.
>
> Villain is a pro but tends to overvalue hands a bit in Pineapple. (Crazy Pineapple is a game where you start with three hole cards and discard one on seeing the flop.)

There are two limps, villain makes it $40, standard for him. There's a call, hero calls in late position with K♦ Q♣ J♦. A blind calls and the limpers call.

The flop is Q♥ J♠ 6♦ and I discard the K♦.

It checks to villain who bets $110. Hero raises to $250 and it folds back to villain, who thinks. As he's tanking, his head is tilted slightly, maybe 10-15 degrees off the vertical. His normal baseline (as with most people) is a non-tilted head. I think a head tilt is a subconscious response: it's a confident person trying to look like they're struggling with a decision. Head tilt isn't that common, but in my experience it's highly reliable for strength. It's kind of like the thinking pose a mathematician might have when someone asks them a tough math problem.

After 45 seconds, villain ships it in.

Without the head tilt, I make the call, as I think he's capable of doing this with overpairs, KT, or QJ. But the head tilt combined with the above-average amount of time he waited made me think it was more likely than usual he had the set.

I fold and Villain showed J♣ J♥ for the set.

Thoughts from Zach: I agree that indicators of thoughtfulness, uncertainty, or displeasure from a bettor make it a lot more likely that a player is relaxed. And a head tilt is a sign of thoughtfulness. *Players who genuinely have a tough decision, or who are bluffing, don't want to let you know they're facing a tough decision.*

Even with medium-strength hands, this pattern would apply. For example: let's consider the villain having AA, which in this spot would be a medium-strength hand. He would instinctually not want to let his opponent know he had something to think about, and would instinctually avoid a thoughtful pose or expression. For one reason: his opponent might have two-pair and still decide to fold, so the player with AA wouldn't want to convey thoughtfulness and make two-pair more likely to call.

Hand #74: Maria Ho gets a neck-pulse read
2007 WSOP $10K Main Event

In 2015, professional player Maria Ho talked to PokerListings.com about a pivotal hand from the 2007 Main Event. In that hand, her opponent's neck pulse after shoving convinced her to make a call. Below, I've paraphrased her interview footage as she tells the story:

> There was a lot of action pre-flop, it was three- or four-bet to me. I had QQ and called. And it was against someone who was very experienced. And on the flop, he put me all in on an 8-high board. And the way he played the hand he could have easily had Aces or Kings.
>
> I remember taking like six or seven minutes. The person was sitting directly to my left. And I looked at them and I was just staring at them the entire time. And I was really just trying to get a live read off of them, because at that point I just had to defer to that.
>
> And I remember so vividly like it was yesterday, his neck just started pulsating. And obviously I could read that as either nervousness or sometimes people are really excited because they have a huge hand. But because he was an experienced pro, I felt like it was more just nervousness, and I felt like the longer I waited him out, the more nervous I sensed his body language to be. And I was fortunate he was sitting right next to me. If he was sitting across from me, maybe I

wouldn't have picked up on these physical tells.

So I called and he flipped over Ace-King.

Thoughts from Zach: Maria makes a few good points here:

- Players betting both strong hands and weak hands are capable of having a fast pulse. People can either be stressed out or excited in a positive way by the situation, both of which can lead to a fast heart rate. It's for this reason that the tell doesn't have much use in a vacuum, as a general tell.

- A fast pulse is more useful as a sign of bluffing and stress for experienced players. This is because *better players have mostly gotten over the excitement of betting strong hands, as that becomes fairly standard over time.* But they are still easily capable of being stressed when making big bluffs, because big bluffs don't happen as often as value-bets. And certain situations, like being deep in a big tournament, are even more likely to get a bluffer's blood pumping.

- Maria took a long time to make her decision. *If her opponent had a decent but not super-strong hand, Maria's tanking would make him more relaxed, not more anxious.* For this reason, a fast pulse after an opponent has tanked for a while increases the chances that it's genuine anxiety.

I will say that I personally have never made a decision based on someone's pulse. Part of this is due to the fact that the behavior can vary so much, especially amongst less experienced competition and at lower stakes. Part of it is probably also due to the fact that I'm a bit red/green color-blind, which means I don't see variations in people's skin tone that well, which means it's kind of hard for me to notice things like pulses and blushing unless I'm very close to someone.

But all that being said, I do believe the pulse can be a valuable tell, especially in high-stakes and high-pressure situations.

Hand #75: Snap-bet on scary board weakens range
$2-5 NLHE cash game

I limp on the button with J♥ 8♠ in a 5-way pot.

The flop is 5♦ 4♠ 4♦. The SB snap-bets $15 into $25.

Again, a snap-bet here makes a 4 less likely than usual. Everyone folds and I call.

The turn is the 4♥, putting three 4s on board.

The SB again snap-bets, betting $40 into $55.

This is a good example of how *scary boards (like paired boards or four-to-a-flush boards) can help in interpreting tells, by polarizing a bettor's hand range.* Bettors will mostly be betting quite strong hands and quite weak hands, and being more cautious with their medium-strength hands.

In this case, it's very unlikely that this player would decide to just snap-bet with quads here. He'd want to think a little bit at the very least, and he'd probably want to convey some uncertainty about the situation. It's going to be very rare for anyone to snap-bet when they've just gotten quads.

I raise to $100, purposefully making the raise small because I thought this would look to him like something

I might do with quads. He folds. If he had called, I would have been making a big bet on the river.

Hand #76: Immediate, small flop raise weakens range
$175 buy-in NLHE tournament

It's early in the tournament and blinds are 100-200. My opponent and I are both pretty deep, with about 16,000 in chips.

I make it 450 in the hijack with A♥ T♦. My opponent calls behind me and we're heads-up to the flop. He's been playing pretty loose pre-flop, but he's hardly been involved at all post-flop. He hasn't seemed willing to call or make significant bets post-flop.

The flop is 8♠ 6♣ 3♠. I bet 500 into 1,200. He immediately raises me to 1,000. My general read for this kind of spot, as you know by now, is that this immediate raise makes sets unlikely. His small min-raise is also another sign of weakness. I think weak-to-medium pairs and flush draws are likely and, based on what I've seen of his play, I think he will lay most of these hands down.

I three-bet to 3,200 and he folds pretty quickly.

If he had called me, I would be willing to bet large on the turn and on the river. Part of my confidence in doing this is that I can credibly represent sets. His behavior makes it unlikely he has a set, and there are many other hands besides sets in his range when he calls my flop raise.

Eye-contact tells from the 2011 WSOP Main Event

One of the most reliable tells I've ever spotted in high-stakes poker footage was a pattern I found on Pius Heinz in the 2011 World Series of Poker Main Event. It was during the heads-up finale between Heinz and Martin Staszko. The final table was televised with a 15-minute delay (as close to live as they can legally make the event), with the hole cards displayed only after the hand was over.

I wanted to watch that event closely because I knew that Heinz, while being an experienced online player, was new to live poker. By all accounts he'd only played a handful of times live. This made me think it was probable that he might have some blind spots in his live poker behavior.

The heads-up match started, and I didn't notice anything for a while. Heinz and Staszko were trying their best to be as stoic as possible, which is true for most players at WSOP Main Event final tables in recent years.

Heinz was an aggressive player. His usual modus operandi was to stare steadily at Staszko, and he did this in most hands where he was the aggressor: before, during, and after betting.

Then a hand played out where Heinz's behavior made me very confident he had a strong hand. Staszko raised. Heinz three-bet. Heinz, instead of the usual steady stare, was mostly looking down at the table, only casting the occasional glance at Staskzo.

Something was very different. I immediately suspected he had AA or KK. *Strong hands are rare, so when you see a player deviate in a big way from his standard behavior, it can be a clue that the player has gotten the rare strong hand.*

It's typically hard to get much of a read pre-flop, due to most players being ambivalent about most hands. But when you *are* able to get a read pre-flop, it'll often be when you read a player for having AA or KK because they do something unusual that gives away their level of relaxation.

Staszko called the three-bet and the flop was 5♦ 4♥ 2♦. Heinz was first to act. Heinz's behavior was even more pronounced here. Instead of the consistent stare, he had his head rested on his arm and was looking down at the table right in front of him. He looked at Staszko for a few seconds, but then went back to looking down. He had a lot more looseness and variety in his gaze direction compared to all the previous spots. So again, I was confident he had a big hand.

He bet the flop and Staskzo folded. Heinz had AA.

Watching the rest of the event, this was a very reliable pattern, as I was able to predict the strength of Heinz's hands from the amount of eye contact he gave Staszko. Steady eye contact during and after betting equaled weakness. Avoiding eye contact when betting, or making intermittent eye contact, equaled some sort of strong hand where he wanted action.

I have two compilations featuring Heinz's behavior on my Youtube channel, at YouTube.com/ReadingPoker-Tells. Search for "Pius Heinz poker tells eye contact" and you'll find the videos. If you're interested in seeing how it played out in practice, I recommend watching the entire heads-up portion of the match. There are several more instances of the pattern in addition to the ones I included in my videos.

As described in my first book, *Reading Poker Tells*, there

are two main eye-related patterns for players making significant bets:

Pattern #1:

- Looking less at an opponent when betting a weak hand (due to being nervous and not wanting to interact)

- Looking more at an opponent when betting with a strong hand (due to being relaxed and not minding interaction)

Pattern #2:

- Looking more at an opponent when betting a weak hand (due to an attempt to convey confidence or intimidate)

- Looking less at an opponent when betting a strong hand (due to wanting to appear meek and unintimidating)

The Pius Heinz pattern fit the second pattern. *But I believe the first pattern is more common for recreational players.* An explanation for this would be that most recreational players are not comfortable bluffing, and don't like to invite observation by looking at their opponent. When recreational players are value-betting strong hands, though, they often enjoy looking towards opponents in order to savor the exhilarating feeling of dominance.

Of course, many players will *not* have a noticeable pattern, either because they'll have a lot of behavioral variation or because they're very consistent in their behavior. But the point is that you can *examine* players and try to find one of the common patterns. This is a very useful read to look for in opponents you regularly face.

Also note: *intermittent, back-and-forth eye contact is much more meaningful a read of relaxation than either direct staring or eye-contact avoidance.* In a vacuum, I'm not likely to have a strong opinion of a bettor who stares directly at an opponent or a bettor who avoids eye contact with an opponent; those behaviors vary so much and need to be correlated first. But when someone changes their gaze direction dynamically and loosely, that's a very strong tell of relaxation, and that's quite reliable even for "cold reads."

A final note: *this pattern, if it exists for a player, is easier to see when two opponents are across the table from each other.* It is less likely to show up or be noticed if players are not sitting across from each other, because players aren't likely to turn and stare at players sitting directly beside them.

Hand #77: Double-check of hole cards from waiting-to-act player
$1-2 NLHE cash game

There are two limps and I limp K♠ T♣ in late position. Another player limps behind me. We're five-way to a flop of Q♣ 9♣ 4♣.

It's checked to me. As I'm getting ready to bet, I see the player behind me double-checking his cards. From a waiting-to-act player this makes the strongest hands unlikely.

I bet $10 into $10. The player behind me quickly makes it $25. Combined with the double-check and the quick raise, this feels like something he would often do with just the A♣ in his hand, or maybe a hand like A♣ 9♠.

Everyone folds and I call the raise with the intention of betting the river if he checks back the turn.

This is a situation where, even if you're confident your opponent has a weak hand, it's not a good idea to raise. On a draw-heavy board like this, it's possible your opponent will be willing to commit a lot of chips with a good draw or a draw combined with a pair. If I had a good 9 or a Queen, a reraise could be justified, but in this spot I'd hate to reraise him and have him shove, which he could easily do with a hand like A♣ 9♠.

This is a good example of how board texture and likely ranges can combine with physical reads to change your decision. *Sometimes, when you have a weak hand and you know an opponent could easily be willing to give you action with a hand that's weak or medium-strength, it's better to wait until later in the hand to try to take the pot down.*

The turn is a blank: the 3♦. I check and he checks back.

The river is the K♥, giving me top pair. The board is Q♣ 9♣ 4♣ 3♦ K♥.

This is kind of interesting. It's likely I have the best hand, and it's likely he probably just had a flush draw on the flop and maybe also a 9 or a 4. If I thought he was a more aggressive player, I would check to him, trying to induce. But he struck me as mostly pretty passive, so I bet $20 into the $60 pot, hoping he might call with a 9. He folded immediately.

Hand #78: Double-check of hole cards before a bet
$5-10 NLHE cash game

There's one limp early. I limp A♦ 8♦ in middle position. An aggressive player raises in late position to $40. The limper and I both call.

The flop is K♥ 8♠ 5♠. The first player and I both check. The pre-flop raiser double-checks his cards and bets $75.

As with a lot of behaviors, *when* a person does something makes a big difference. A double-check immediately before a significant bet is much different than a double-check from a player who is waiting for the player in front of him to act.

A double-check that happens right before a bet makes it likely the player is not bluffing. Double-checking cards could potentially communicate a player was uncertain about what he had, and uncertainty could be read as weakness. Bluffers don't want to accidentally convey weakness and make an opponent suspicious; for this reason bluffers are unlikely to double-check their cards right before a bluff.

If a player needed to actually double-check what his cards were, he would usually do so right before or after cards coming out; this is when players pay less attention to opponents, and that's why most genuine double-checks of hole cards happen at those times.

It's worth emphasizing that we're talking specifically about double-checks that happen *immediately before a bet.* Not double-checks that happen before checking. And not double-checks that happen before it's a player's turn to act.

Keep in mind a double-check doesn't necessarily mean

a very strong hand; it just makes a bluff unlikely. You will see it done a good amount with decent but not great hands.

In this situation, I'd usually be calling this player's flop bet, just because he's known for being very aggressive and pretty bad. But with this small clue, I decide to fold.

Again, folding early in a hand is never that big a mistake, so even if I'm wrong sometimes it's not a big deal.

I fold, telling him that I almost called. He said he had K♠ J♠, and I believed him.

Double-check of hole cards in 2015 WSOP

In the 13th episode of the 2015 WSOP Main Event coverage, there were two notable hands where the same player double-checked his hole cards before a bet or raise. The player was Pierre Neuville, who went on to make the final table and get 7th place.

In one hand, Pierre Neuville raised with A♠ 2♣ and was called by Josh Beckley. The flop came K♥ 8♣ 4♠, and Beckley check-called Neuville's continuation bet. The turn was the 2♥. Beckley checked and Neuville checked back. The river brought the 2♠, giving Neuville trips. Beckley bet and Neuville double-checked his cards before raising.

Later on in the same episode, Neuville got into a blind-vs-blind battle and four-bet from the SB with K♣ 6♣. On a flop of K♦ T♦ 7♠, Neuville double-checked his cards before betting. (Again: the double-check before a bet won't necessarily mean a very strong hand; it just makes a bluff unlikely.)

Norman Chad mentioned the behavior, saying, "This is the second time tonight we've seen Pierre look back at his cards after hitting one of them to make sure he has what he has."

In fairness to Neuville, it's entirely possible that he is balanced with this behavior and the producers showed only the hands in which he did this when strong. But I think it's more likely he was imbalanced.

Hand #79: Weak-hand statement strengthens bettor's range

$2-5 NLHE cash game

I played this hand when I was doing research for my *Verbal Poker Tells* book and talking a lot more at the table than I usually do.

I raised pre-flop to $20 with A♥ Q♥. I got two callers.

The flop was K♣ Q♠ 5♠. The first player checked, I checked, and the player behind me bet $35 into $65. The first player folded and it was on me.

I asked the bettor, "You got Ace-King?"

He responded quickly, "No."

As discussed, weak-hand statements (i.e., statements that remove strong hands from a player's range) make strong hands significantly more likely, and this is true whether you induce them or a player says them of his own accord. Players betting weak hands do not want to weaken their range, because they're generally worried about accidentally inducing action. This was a very direct example of a weak-hand statement. I folded and the bettor showed 5♣ 5♦ for a set.

Most recreational players have no clue about how much meaning these seemingly minor statements can contain, which is why these statements are so consistently reliable.

Hand #80: Joking statements and small raise contain clues

$5-10 NLHE cash game

There's an UTG limp. UTG+1, who we'll call Dave, makes it $30. He has about $600 to start the hand. Dave is usually loose-passive and not often aggressive.

His raise size here is a very reliable tell of weakness for him. With one limp in front of him, he'd almost always be raising more than 3x with big pairs or AK/AQ.

I make it $85 on the button with Q♥ Q♣. I purposefully size it a bit smaller than I usually would to make a call from him more likely.

The SB, who's been playing pretty tightly, calls after a long pause. I put him on JJ or TT, maybe AK. Dave calls.

The flop is 6♦ 5♣ 5♠.

Dave checks. I bet $150 into $265. After a long pause, the SB calls.

Dave starts moving around in an animated way. He gives a little speech that goes on for a while, and it includes him saying, "Might as well put it in." He then puts in $400, keeping only like $110 behind. He jokingly says something about how he's saving the rest for a cab ride home.

There are two interesting things here:

- The weak-hand statements
- The small bet-sizing

Almost all weak-hand statements accompanying significant bets will be said with strong hands. If this player were bluffing, he'd be unlikely to want to convey weakness by saying, "Might as well put it in," because that implies some uncertainty and ambivalence about his hand. He'd also be unlikely, even jokingly, to imply he might need a cab ride home after losing the hand. (Joking statements, though, are generally less reliable than serious statements, just because they are intended to not be taken seriously.) So his verbal behavior is supporting evidence for him having a strong hand.

This player is mostly loose-passive, especially post-flop. Given this, it would be rare for him to want to stack off with a vulnerable hand (like 77-JJ) versus two players who've already shown interest. This is more evidence for him having a strong hand.

Regarding the bet-sizing: if a player were going to raise in this spot with a medium-strength overpair, a draw, or any other vulnerable hand, it's unlikely he would make such a small raise, from $150 to $400, and hold back $100. Most players with a vulnerable hand or bluff, with a decent-sized pot and a short stack, are just going to put all the money in, either out of frustration or to maximize fold equity. This is more evidence for him having a very strong hand.

On the other side of things: he rarely has a 5 in his hand, considering he raised early and then called my three-bet. Decent players and tight players would basically never have a lone 5 here, especially with only 60 BBs to start the hand, but Dave was capable of occasionally doing weird things like calling here with A5 suited or 65 suited or something. Still, even considering this, it'd still be rare for him.

It's possible for him to have 66 for the flopped boat. But I think he would usually not raise with it on the flop. But if he did decide to raise with it, I think he'd usually be more cagey and thoughtful in his demeanor.

All things considered: there were very few hands that beat me, but at the same time his line and behavior seemed strong to me.

Another factor was that he was so short-stacked. Considering the size of the pot and the amount I had to call, I basically had to be around 90% sure that he had me beat to fold here.

I ended up calling fairly quickly without thinking about it very much, and of course calling the remaining $100 on the turn. He turned over 5♦ 3♦, for trip 5s.

Thinking more about it after the hand, I think all of the evidence points very reliably towards a strong hand. If it were just the line and bet-sizing, or just the relaxed, hand-range-weakening verbal behavior, I wouldn't be so sure, but both of them combined seem to almost certainly indicate strength. If I could play this hand over again, I would fold.

I posted this hand on the poker forum *TwoPlusTwo.com* and someone made this comment:

"Are you actually advocating folding an overpair in a three-bet pot when dude opens originally and flats your three-bet after starting with 60bb? Do you realize how truly awful this is?"

I include this comment because it shows some of the antipathy some players have toward the idea of using reads. The only reason I thought this hand was worthy of discussion was precisely because it was a tough decision due to the shallow stack size.

But I'm confident that the behavior and bet-sizing in this hand dramatically strengthen this player's range, and I'm also confident that most experienced live players would agree with me. If you accept that this is true, then the question then becomes: *How confident are we in this read?* Are we confident enough to fold in such a shallow spot? Or are we not certain enough in our read and so have to call? The answer to this boils down to some things that are hard to quantify, like:

- What we've seen of a player's past behavior
- Our own subjective read of the situation and the behavior

So it's hard to make confident statements like "We should always call here" or "We should always fold here." I do believe it's beneficial to think about these things and to not have set-in-stone thinking like, "We're *x* BBs deep with an overpair and always have to get it in." Paying more attention to small clues and recognizing spots where you might have more information than you initially think will help you in the long run.

We'll look at two more hands featuring the verbal behavior of Dave, the player from the last hand. My goal is to show how you can form a read over time when playing a lot with the same player. The main general read I had on Dave was that he was prone to talking more, and talking in a more agitated way, when betting weak, vulnerable hands. When he was betting a strong hand, he was likely to either stay silent, or make calm, weak-hand statements.

Hand #81: Dave's verbal clues encourage call

$2-5 NLHE cash game

Two players limp, I call in late position with 8♠ 7♠. Behind me, Dave raises to $30. He had just lost a hand to me and only has $250 to start this hand. I get the feeling he's kind of tilty, especially towards me.

Another player and I call.

The flop is 9♣ 7♥ 4♠. The first player checks and I bet $45 into $90.

Dave quickly shoves for $175 more. The other player folds and action returns to me.

Dave is usually pretty tight and passive, but he is capable of doing random weird things. I think he will usually, with his raise here, have at least a bigger pair.

I ask Dave, "Did you raise pre-flop?"

He says, "Yeah" pretty quickly.

The literal meaning of Dave's response is to remind me that he raised pre-flop. If Dave had flopped a set or had a big pair, I know he'd very much want to get action, and I know he'd likely be more cagey or deceptive. *If he had a strong hand, I don't think he'd often remind me that he was the pre-flop raiser.* In other words: he has less motivation to remind me that his range is stronger than normal, because doing so could influence me to fold. At the same time, players betting strong hands can be relaxed and do all sorts of strange stuff, so this behavior isn't super reliable, but it does make the strongest hands a bit less likely than usual.

Then he says, "It doesn't matter" and laughs. This fits the general pattern that I've noticed hold true for him over several months: him being more talkative and exuberant when holding a weak hand. Unlike the weak-hand statements in the last hand, the "it doesn't matter" can be seen as a strong-hand statement, conveying comfort with my potential call.

This combination of information makes up my mind and I call. He has K♣ Q♣, just King-high.

Hand #82: More verbal clues from Dave

$2-5 NLHE cash game

I raise to $20 early with A♠ J♥. There are two callers, one of them Dave in the SB. He only has $235 to start the hand.

The flop is 9♥ 6♣ 3♠. They both check and I bet $35 into $62. Dave check-raises to $85 and the third player folds. He only has $130 left.

As I survey his stack, Dave says, "I can't fold, I've only got like $100 left, I can't fold." This seems defensive. Dave would often agitatedly ramble when bluffing, and that behavior was different than the relaxed "I don't have much" kind of statements he'd sometimes make with strong hands. At the same time, he might feel defensive here with any pair.

I don't think he would usually check-raise like this with a 9 or a 6. It's possible, but I think usually he'd just call the $35 and hope for me to check back the turn. If he were going to check-raise me with a 9, I think he'd usually raise a little bigger. This raise strikes me like something he could easily do with open-ended draws: 8-7 or 5-4.

I ask him, "You have eight-seven?"

He laughs for a few seconds and smiles at me. He seems genuinely amused, which is how I'd expect him to act if I'd actually guessed his hand. Sometimes when you name a player's hand exactly, they'll be a little caught off-guard and let a little genuine amusement slip.

Then he says, "You got an overpair? If you had an overpair, you'd snap call."

This again seems defensive to me. As I said, he likes to verbally ramble when betting weak hands.

I decide to shove. It's not that I'm super-confident he has 8-7 or 5-4, it's more that I think he has hands like that often enough to make this slightly +EV for me. Also, if he does have a weak pair, or a draw with some equity, there's a chance he folds to my shove. It was definitely a borderline decision on my part, though.

He calls my shove for his remaining $130. He shows 8♠ 7♠. My Ace-high holds up.

This call had some meta-value for me. Dave occasionally brought this hand up for the next few months, telling people about my insanity and saying he'd never try to bluff me again. The potential meta-value and advertising value was one extra reason I made what I thought was such a borderline play.

Hand #83: Honest statements help define range

$1-2 NLHE cash game

It's a raised multi-way hand. One of the pre-flop callers bets out on an A♣ K♥ T♥ flop and everyone folds.

The next hand, there's a $5 UTG straddle. Someone raises to $15 and three people call, including the player who bet the flop in the last hand.

Before the flop comes, this player says, "Same flop." I thought she was being honest with this wish because she is often honest and not cautious with her words.

The flop is K♥ 9♣ 6♠. The pre-flop raiser checks and the "same flop" player bets $35 second-to-act.

If we assume that she's being honest about wanting the same flop (A-K-T), and if we know that she doesn't like to bet draws, it has become very likely that she has either K-T or AK. If we also happen to know that she doesn't like to three-bet AK, then she's equally likely to have either AK or KT.

But we also know there was an early pre-flop raiser who checked the flop; there's an above average chance this player has an Ace in his hand, which makes it a bit more likely the "same flop" player has K-T and not AK.

Obviously, being able to pin down this player to such a specific range could have practical implications if you were going to continue in the hand.

She did have K♣ T♥.

It's good to notice how players' verbal behavior shows up. This one may seem like a minor, fairly rare tell, but you might be surprised how often recreational live players do these kinds of things. The player in this hand was a

$2-5 and $5-10 regular who often played multiple days a week, and who often gave away her hands with these kinds of verbal leaks. Taking her verbal behavior seriously, and taking time to analyze it, gave me a large edge on her.

Hand #84: An attempt at a reverse verbal tell

$5-10 NLHE cash game

In a 6-way limped pot, the flop is 6♣ 4♥ 2♥.

Fourth-to-act, a player leads out for $50 into $60 and says, "Okay, I'll see where I'm at."

For inexperienced players, such a weak-hand statement will usually indicate a strong hand. This player, however, is fairly experienced. While he's not a good player, he has played a lot. When I heard this statement, I immediately suspected it was a second-level deception (i.e., a false tell), said truthfully with a weak hand. In other words: this player was experienced enough to not make this statement in an obvious, weak-means-strong way.

In *Verbal Poker Tells*, I explain that *the more common a phrase is, the more likely it will be used for reverse-tell purposes.* "I'll see where I'm at" is one such phrase that is said a lot. Another example is "Let's gamble." Because it's a common phrase, and commonly understood to indicate a strong hand, it becomes more likely that experienced players will use it in the opposite way.

In this hand, this player got one caller, checked on the turn, and folded to his opponent's bet.

Hand #85: Same verbal tell from same player
$5-10 NLHE cash game

This hand is from a few weeks after the last hand.

The same player from the last hand raises early to $25. There's one call and I call on the button with J♠ T♠.

The flop is 7♣ 7♦ 4♦.

The pre-flop raiser says, "Ok, I'll see where I'm at right away," and bets $50 into $90. The second player folds.

Based on this behavior, which I'd seen him do with weak hands a couple times in the past, I call. I decide not to raise because if he has a flush draw, which is quite possible, he may be committed to a lot more action, and may even reraise me.

The turn is the K♠. He checks and I bet $130 into $190.

He shows 3♦ 3♣ and folds.

Over the course of several months playing with this player, he said this same phrase in four spots that I noticed, all of them when bluffing.

Hand #86: Call for card contains clues
$2-5 NLHE cash game

A pretty passive and tight player limps early and ends up calling a $20 raise. Four players see a flop of Q♣ 9♠ 7♥.

The pre-flop raiser makes a small bet: $20 into $80. One player calls and then the tight player calls last-to-act.

Before the turn comes, the tight player calls for a card, shouting, "Ten!"

Let's examine this statement.

We know that most verbal behavior from non-aggressors will make weak hands likely. With this call-for-a-card, sets have become unlikely.

Also, players who actually have a decent draw are unlikely to call for the card they need, as they don't want to scare away action if they do hit.

This becomes less true for very unlikely hands. For example, it's entirely possible this player might call out, "Two!" if he had pocket 2s, because he knows a) it's unlikely to happen, b) people aren't likely to believe him because it's so disconnected from the board, and c) his hand would still be far from the nuts. But for normal straight and flush draws, and higher sets, it's unlikely for a person to call for the card they actually need.

His call for "Ten" means that the straight draws (KJ, J-8, and 8-6) have all become unlikely. Q-T is also unlikely, as he wouldn't want to draw attention to top two pair. Besides, all of these hands are unlikely from a fundamental perspective, as we know this player is tight and that he limped early and called a raise.

What else do we know? We know that players who call for cards often do so truthfully, but in an indirect (often slightly humorous) way.

What hand would a Ten help in this case, but not help directly?

A hand containing a Jack is one possibility: if he had AJ or QJ or JJ or J-9, a Ten would give him an open-ended straight draw. Many calls for cards are indirectly truthful in this way, with the player, in a somewhat humorous manner, calling for a card that will give them more outs. Also, if the card *does* come, it might scare the speaker's opponents and slow them down, which is another reason people like to do this: free-rolling for a free card.

The turn arrives and the board is Q♣ 9♠ 7♥ T♣.

The tight player is second-to-act and he bets out $40 into the $140 pot.

If you were an opponent in this hand (and ignoring the other players), *this player's verbal behavior should encourage you to raise him.* Because he is likely to have a straight draw here, there's a good chance he'll call a raise that's not very large, so you could size it smaller if you wanted a call. If he calls the turn raise, it's very likely he'll be folding on the river if he doesn't improve.

Another interesting thing about this hand: if we knew that this player was very passive and not the type to bet only a straight draw here, we could also surmise it's likely that he picked up a flush draw. Having an open-ended straight draw and a flush draw, and having just requested a card that actually arrived: all of this could influence a usually passive, tight player to take a out-of-character stab at the pot.

Having played with this player a lot, I guessed that he most probably had both a straight and a flush draw here, and knowing he limped early and called a raise, I thought A♣ J♣ was very probable. Sure, he had to call a flop bet with only runner-runner possibilities, but that wasn't hard to believe for even a tight player. He had three cards to a royal flush and he only had to call a small $20 flop bet, which also closed the action in a $120 pot.

Everyone folded to this player's bet and he showed A♣ J♣.

Hand #87: Bettor confusion strengthens range
$5-10 NLHE cash game

A loose, aggressive, and very bad player raises UTG to $40. Two players call and I call in the BB with K♣ J♣.

The flop is A♥ A♦ J♥. The SB and I both check.

The pre-flop raiser acts confused and looks back and forth from me to the small blind. He says, "Oh, you checked?" Then he bets $60 into $160.

Any confusion from a bettor makes a strong hand more likely, even something as seemingly innocuous as this. If this player were betting a weak hand here, he'd want to do so normally and straightforwardly. These small communications of confusion and uncertainty will usually show up from someone who's very relaxed.

This is especially true when the thing the player seems confused about is very clear. In this case, there was no ambiguity about my check or the small blind's check, and the pre-flop raiser was sitting directly beside us, seemingly paying attention. If he had perhaps been talking to a waitress or something when we checked, his confusion could be logically explained, but in this case it was unlikely that he wouldn't have noticed we checked.

The other players fold and I fold, too. This player was very loose and bad and normally I'd always make this call, but this player's behavior dramatically increased the chances he had an Ace.

After I folded, he showed A♠ Q♦.

Something to note about this behavior, and many behaviors like it: this kind of behavior isn't necessarily a conscious act. I don't think most instances of players doing things like this are conscious attempts at deception. I think it's mostly unconscious: an instinct to portray some timidity or uncertainty when in a position of power. This helps explain why many of these small leaks of strength or defensiveness are common: it's not that so many poker players are trying to be deceptive, *it's just that it's instinctive and natural for people in competitive situations to act in a way that seems opposite of their true status.*

Hand #88: Player-specific bet-timing read
$5-10 NLHE cash game

A player raises to $35 in late position. I call in the BB with 8♣ 4♣. This isn't something I would normally do, but I have a good read on this player, built up over many months, and so I do look for reasons to get into pots with him.

The flop is A♣ T♠ 5♣, giving me a flush draw.

I check. My opponent takes a long time to gather chips, looking at me and then down at his chips, stacking up chips into two piles. Eventually he makes a pot-sized bet of $75.

The main read I have on this player is that he usually takes a long time to gather chips and bet when he's betting weak hands. Whereas when he has a strong hand, he just bets normally, in a fairly quick, efficient manner. This is the opposite of a common general tell: having *more* hesitation when betting strong hands.

If I had to try to explain the motivations behind this tell, I would say: When this player is considering betting weak hands, he's somewhat anxious. He's more likely to stall and try to get a sense of his opponent's demeanor, and see if he can maybe sense some weakness. Whereas when he's got an actual hand, he's more relaxed and doesn't have as much to think about and he just throws the bet out in a more normal fashion.

I check-raise him to $200 and he folds.

The tell was quite reliable but not super-reliable, so I do want some possibilities when I do this. I wouldn't make this move with air.

Hand #89: Another bet-timing read on same player
$2-5 NLHE cash game

Here's another hand with the same player.

I'm the pre-flop raiser with J♦ J♥ and I hit top set on a flop of J♣ 7♣ 5♣.

My opponent bets into me on the flop and turn. On the turn, he takes a long time to assemble and put his chips in, betting $45 into $65. As in the last hand, I know that his long pauses make weak hands significantly more likely.

If it weren't for this read, I would have to play the hand cautiously. But because I'm confident it's unlikely he has a flush, I raise to $145. He calls. On a blank river, I bet and he folds.

Hand #90: Jennifer Harman gets a read on Bellande
2005 WSOP $10,000 NLHE Circuit event

In a 2005 $10K buy-in WSOP Circuit event, Jennifer Harman got 2nd place. Several years later, she talked about a tell she got from her opponent Jean-Robert Bellande.

Bellande had 9♥ 7♣. Harman had J♥ 7♦. The flop was K♦ 7♠ 5♣.

Harman: *Jean-Robert plays aggressive and he will bet with nothing, so when he bet on the flop, I called to see what he was going to do on the turn.*

The turn is a 3♠. Bellande bets.

Harman: *When he bet on the turn, there was something, the way he bet, clicked in my brain, that I had him beat. Jean-Robert bets pretty fast, and there was a small pause on the turn that he had that just didn't ring true for Jean-Robert's style.*

The river is the 8♥. Bellande bets.

Harman: *I made the decision that if I was calling him on the turn, I was calling him on the river. That's why it's so important to stay focused in a poker game because there are so many subtleties you'll miss if you don't.*

While it's not very clear, I think what Harman is saying is: because Bellande typically bets fast in most spots, including with his strong hands, she interpreted his pause on the turn as indicating some actual uncertainty from him.

While I believe Jennifer Harman is probably quite skilled at reading poker tells, it's possible her skill is mostly subconscious, and not specifically organized consciously. Supporting evidence for this is that she says that something "clicked in [her] brain" to make her think Bellande was weak; she doesn't explicitly describe reasons behind the read. I think it's possible some successful high-stakes players don't have a fully conscious understanding of why they do some things.

Another explanation is that she actually has a solid read on Bellande, but doesn't want to explain it too specifically because she was still often playing with him.

Hand #91: Chip-flipping tell in the 2011 WSOP

During the heads-up finale of the 2011 WSOP Main Event, Martin Staszko was very stoic. His behavior was very consistent from hand to hand and he was, as far as I could tell, largely unreadable.

There was one hand, though, where his behavior made me very confident he had a strong hand.

Heinz raises to 3.4M and Staszko calls. The flop is A♦ 9♠ 3♦.

Staszko checks. Heinz bets 3.8M. Staszko calls.

The turn is the A♠. Staszko checks. Heinz bets 8.4M into 14.8M.

This is where it gets interesting. Staszko waits about 25 seconds, then starts gathering chips in front of him. He pulls over enough for a call, so it looks like he's preparing to call. Then he pauses, looking back at Heinz several times, as if thinking. Then he starts to flip a chip, end over end, on top of his chip stack. He does a complete flip of the chip 14 times. Then he starts to gather chips again, this time pulling over more chips from his other stacks that were previously off to the side. He raises to 18.5M.

There are two interesting behaviors here:

- Flipping a chip before raising

- Pauses or hesitations before a bet/raise

Both of these behaviors will make strong hands more likely. Let's look at each of them.

Flipping a chip is what some behavior analysts call a "gravity-defying" behavior. People who are relaxed tend to have more upward-directed movements that "defy gravity." Examples of gravity-defying behaviors in everyday life include: raising eyebrows, raising arms in triumph, and bouncing legs up and down. *People who are anxious are more restrained in their behavior and are unlikely to have these loose, upward motions.*

When it comes to playing with chips, there will be a good amount of variety. Some players play with their chips a lot; you've probably played with players who riffle their chips constantly. For a lot of the more common and consistent behaviors, it will be hard to find a pattern.

Flipping a chip end over end, though, is an especially loose and playful behavior. When associated with a bet, I think it's a generally reliable sign of relaxation, more so than the more common chip riffling. But I wouldn't read too much into it unless I'd been able to watch a player for a while to see how it might be showing up. For example, if Staszko were constantly flipping chips before making bets or raises, it wouldn't be likely to have any meaning.

But, as I've said, Staszko was very stoic. This was the first time in the match that I'd seen him play with his chips in such a way when associated with a bet or a raise. (He did sometimes flip chips in non-aggressor spots.) Because he had been so stoic and restrained in his behavior prior to this, his chip-flipping in this hand, followed by his raise, made it likely it was a small but reliable leak of relaxation with a strong hand. If he were bluffing or making a raise with a vulnerable hand, it's unlikely he'd have this playful, gravity-defying behavior.

Let's consider the pause in his chip-gathering.

Bluffers like to convey confidence and certainty. For this reason, they're unlikely to have pauses and hesitations in their chip gathering. Players betting strong hands, conversely, can have a motivation to seem uncertain, which can lead to some hesitating behaviors. Also, players with strong hands may be considering the best bet-sizing, which can also lead to hesitating behaviors.

If Staszko were bluffing here, he wouldn't want to—purposefully or accidentally—seem uncertain about whether to raise. If he were going to bluff, he'd just want to put the raise in all at one time in a neutral way. He wouldn't want to potentially make Heinz suspicious by looking like he was going to call and then seeming to change his mind.

When I saw both of these behaviors from Staszko here, and knowing how stoic he'd been up to that point, I was very confident he had a strong hand.

Heinz didn't have the same opinion, though. He called the raise with, as we learned after the hand, 7♣ 6♠, just 7 high, no draw.

On the river, Staszko bet 20M into 52M and Heinz folded. Staszko had A♣ 9♣, for the turned full house.

Hand #92: Post-bet leg-bounce clue of strength

$2-5 NLHE cash game

A loose, strange, sometimes-aggressive player raises to $20 in mid-position. I have A♦ T♦ and call on the button. The BB calls.

The flop is T♠ 7♣ 6♣. The PFR bets $40 and I call.

The turn is the 3♦. The PFR bets $90 into $142.

His physical demeanor after betting is loose. He looks at me and around the table loosely. He is sitting two seats away from me and I can see that his leg is bouncing under the table.

Leg bouncing is another "gravity-defying" behavior that will tend to indicate relaxation. In the absence of any player-specific history to the contrary, it's a good general indicator of a strong hand. For this specific player, I'd played with him a good amount and I'd seen him bounce his leg when betting a strong hand a few times in the past.

If it weren't for this behavior, I'd be calling this bet. But I'm confident enough in the leg bouncing tell that I'll fold any close-to-borderline hands.

Hand #93: Bettor's stillness weakens range

$2-5 NLHE cash game

I raise to $20 with A♥ A♣ and get three callers.

The flop is Q♠ T♥ 7♣. I bet $60 into $87. I get one caller: the player behind me. He's a very tight, fit-or-fold type player. He's got $400 behind and I cover.

The turn is the 3♦. I check and my opponent bets $130 into $207.

This is not a fun spot. I'm definitely calling the bet, but not loving it. And if this player makes a big river bet, I'm almost certainly beat.

I think AQ and KQs are pretty much the only hands he bets with here that I beat. I have two Aces, so there are only six combinations of AQ, and three combinations of KQs (he doesn't call my raise with KQo pre-flop). I think he has all sets in his range, and there are nine combos of flopped sets. So 9 combinations of hands I beat and 9 combos of hands that beat me.

I watch him for a while. He's very still. He stays staring

at the middle of the table, toward the cards. He's sitting next to me and I keep staring at him, seeing if he'll give me some eye contact or movement, but he doesn't.

I've played with this guy a good amount. When he's betting strong hands, he's more relaxed: he has normal small movements and is capable of looking around and at opponents. Here, though, he is super-still. I think this is entirely fitting with the anxiety he'd feel betting AQ here: he wouldn't like the situation.

Without my read, I'd only call this bet. But because I think it's more likely he's on the more anxious side, I shove for his remaining $270. He thinks a long time and calls. He has A♦ Q♥.

The main point here is that *this is a player-specific read.* I would never try to read much into stillness against a player who was a stranger to me. Many players are consistently still after making large bets, so it'd be a mistake to read much into that behavior. But I'd played with this player and knew he often had small movements and was more physically loose when betting strong hands.

Hand #94: Bettor's gulp makes bluff more likely
$500 buy-in NLHE tournament

Waiting for a tournament, I was playing a $2-5 cash game. Also playing was Jeff Dobrin, a cash game pro and WSOP Circuit Ring winner. We got to talking. I ended up telling him that I'd written a book on poker tells, something I usually don't bring up when I play because it can lead to weird during-hand interactions.

Flash forward a few hours later: we're in the third or

fourth level of the $500 tournament. Jeff gets a table change and comes to our table, two seats to my right. A few hands in, he raises in late position and I three-bet with A♣ 3♦ on the button. He calls.

The flop comes 9♥ 6♠ 4♣. He checks and I bet. Jeff calls rather quickly. The turn is the T♥. Jeff checks. I make a large bet, around 1/2 of my remaining stack.

Jeff considers, and smiles a bit. He says, "Why so much? It feels like you really don't want a call here."

I might have smiled back. And then, because I was a bit nervous, I gulped.

He chuckles and says: "The 'Big Gulp', huh? From the guy who wrote the book on poker tells? No way."

I do have a tendency of gulping when I'm bluffing. I don't have alligator blood; I'm a pretty anxious person in general. I adjust the best way I know how: I try to balance this known pattern by swallowing after betting big hands, too. But this long-term balancing didn't help me here, in the moment, if Jeff was going to follow through on his read.

"I don't know what you're talking about," I say in an overly innocent tone, like I'm trying to be funny while obviously knowing what he's talking about. Basically it was an instinctual attempt to try to appear relaxed with the situation; some desperate damage control.

"That's just too obvious," Jeff says. He thinks a few seconds. "You have to be doing that on purpose." The thing I had going for me was that he knew I wrote a book on poker tells, so maybe he'd give me credit for a false tell.

Finally he says, "You might be trying to trick me with that." He folds his pocket deuces face up. I show the bluff. He shakes his head.

"Oh, the gulp was real! I thought you had to be leveling me with that," he says.

"I could have been," I say, trying to seem more complex than I actually am.

A gulp, also known as a "hard swallow," is generally associated with nervousness and fear. You've probably been in a situation where anxiety makes your throat constrict, giving you that "lump in the throat" feeling and that desire to swallow.

In poker, things get more complicated. You can find many instances of players gulping after betting with a wide range of hands. As with many behaviors, gulping isn't easily nailed down to a specific hand strength.

When writing my poker tells column for Bluff Magazine, I talked to poker player Daniel Steinberg. Daniel is a professional poker player, and is the twin brother of pro player Max Steinberg (4th in the 2015 WSOP ME). Daniel's also a keen observer of behavior at the poker table. Daniel had this to say on the subject:

"I don't tend to assign much importance to it. At a tournament recently, there was a player who gulped after making a large river bet and he had a strong hand. You would think gulping would be a sign of nervousness so would generally be correlated to bluffs. But I think it can also be a sign of worry about losing a big pot with a semi-strong hand."

That's one point. Another point is that many players gulp frequently. When I was doing live analysis of the 2013 WSOP Main Event final table, I had a poker friend text me that he thought one of the players, Marc-Etienne McLaughlin, was gulping when he was betting weak hands. But actually, McLaughlin was balanced with his gulping and was doing it pretty frequently, with all hand strengths. Perhaps, like me, he was balancing his known tendency to gulp when anxious by consciously gulping in other spots. *If you do something frequently, and do it in diverse situations, you won't have a pattern that will be easy to notice.*

One other factor: some players use gulping as a false tell, to try to deceptively communicate weakness to an opponent. I have talked to a few experienced players who have used it consciously when betting a strong hand, to try to get a call.

A few months after my hand versus Jeff Dobrin, I emailed Jeff to ask him for his thoughts on gulping and swallowing. He had this to say:

> I think gulping during or immediately after a bet isn't reliable as an indicator on its own, because it can mean strength or weakness. I find the gulp to be most useful when you try to elicit it with an interaction. I'm a big believer in talking to opponents in key spots and studying them during this interaction. Sometimes confronting your opponent with an unexpected piece of information will elicit a physical reaction. In this context, an immediate and reflexive gulp is almost always a sign of anxiety.
>
> An example: In a recent $2-5 game, I have pocket fives and hit bottom set versus a pre-flop raiser on a K♠ 9♠ 5♥ flop. I lead out and he min-raises me, so there's a slight possibility that he could have flopped a higher set. On a 7♦ turn, I check-raise him to $155, and he shoves for the rest of his stack, about $375 more, which I cover.
>
> While I'm probably not folding a set here, there's also no harm in trying to get a little information. So I ask, "Would

you really play Aces this way? I've got a set." This elicits a strong gulp from him that I feel is genuine nervousness. This makes me feel much better about making the call. He shows pocket Aces. And knowing how he reacted in that spot can be useful for tough spots later on.

Hand #95: A fake gulp

2009 WSOP $10K NLHE Main Event

On a river of K♣ 7♠ 5♠ T♠ A♥, pro player Peter Jetten bets and his opponent, Phil Ivey, considers.

Jetten gulps.

Ivey says, "You put the fake swallow on me?"

Ivey eventually calls. Jetten shows A♦ 5♥ for two pair. Ivey mucks.

Both Ivey and Jetten are experienced players. Ivey's statement here is a good example of the kind of thoughts you can have when there's some unusual behavioral information and both you and your opponent are experienced players. You have to ask yourself questions like: "Is the gulp a real sign of nervousness? I know he's a good player, so is it possible he's just acting nervous to get me to call?"

When two opponents are both good players, any out-of-the-ordinary behavior can create tricky, confusing situations.

Hand #96: Attempt at reverse verbal tell

$1-2 NLHE cash game

We're five-way to the flop for $9 each. I'm on the button with A♥ 3♥.

The flop is T♥ 8♦ 4♥. The pre-flop raiser and two

other players check. The player in front of me bets $45
into $48. He has $160 behind. He's a fairly experienced
player, but also tight and cautious. I think hands like AT
and JJ are probable. His large bet-sizing also makes me
think sets are unlikely.

I shove for $200, saying, "If you got me, you got me."

Because this player is fairly experienced and takes the
game seriously, I think there's a good chance he will
interpret my statement as a sign of strength. I'm imitating
a small faux-uncertain misdirection a recreational player
might say with a strong hand.

If he does have a big hand, my behavior's probably not
going to make a difference; he'll be calling. But if he has
a hand he's not that excited about, like QT or AT, maybe
even JJ, there's a chance my statement might get him to fold.

I don't often try to do these kinds of tricky false tells.
Generally I think it's hard to predict how players will
interpret your behavior. And if you do it more than
once to the same opponent, you'll wind up in confusing
"leveling wars" where you don't know where you stand.

I do occasionally do these kinds of things if I think my
opponent is a thinking, somewhat-experienced player
and likely to recognize common tells. Generally I'd just
be using the behavior to add slightly to my chances of
getting a fold or getting a call; I don't go too far out on a
limb with the false tell. In other words, I'll attempt it in
spots like this: where I think it won't negatively affect me
much if my deception doesn't work.

After I shove, everyone folds back to the first bettor.
He thinks a while and says, "I'm not falling for that. I'm
folding." He shows A♦ T♣ for top pair.

Hand #97: Tight player's snap-call defines range
$5-10 NLHE cash game

It's limped around four-way. I'm in the BB with K♥ J♦. The flop is J♣ 5♥ 4♦. The SB and I check.

The UTG limper, who often stabs at pots when checked to, bets $25 into the $40 pot very quickly and forcefully. Quick, forceful bets, when the pot is small, will tend to make the strongest hands less likely, so it's less likely than usual that he has a set or an overpair.

The SB, a tight, cautious player, calls. I make it $85. The UTG player folds quickly. The SB calls immediately.

This snap-call is interesting. What can we say about it? We know that snap calls make the strongest hands unlikely. In this situation, it's unlikely this player has a set or two-pair.

But because this player is tight, we know that the hand can't be too weak, either. In the moment, AJ was really the only hand I could imagine this player snap-calling with in this spot. With KJ or weaker, he'd want to consider the situation for at least a few seconds. With pairs weaker than a Jack: same thing, he'd want to think a little. A straight draw of any kind, he'd have to think, and probably end up folding.

Sometimes immediate calls from an opponent will be useful in encouraging you to bluff. But a lot of that will depend on an opponent's playing style, their chip stack, and other factors. In this case, this player only had about $500 behind, so I thought there was a good chance he'd go the whole way with AJ. I also thought my weird check-raise line might have made him suspicious. For both reasons, I wasn't motivated to try to turn my KJ into a bluff.

The turn was the 5♦, pairing the 5. He checked and I checked back.

The river board was J♣ 5♥ 4♦ 5♦ Q♠. He paused a while and checked. I checked back.

He showed A♥ J♠ and took the pot.

This hand is a good example of how a player's looseness/tightness will affect how you interpret and make use of behavioral info. If this player had been a loose player and had called my flop raise immediately, there'd be plenty of medium-strength hands in his range and I would have been encouraged to value-bet. But because this player was tight, I thought he had a narrow and pretty strong snap-calling range.

Hand #98: Discussing tells with regular opponents

$2-5 NLHE cash game

This hand shows why it can be confusing and bad for you to talk strategy with players you play with frequently. As a general rule, I don't talk strategy with regular opponents, but occasionally I find myself breaking that rule.

My opponent in this hand is a strong, observant player. A few weeks previously, he'd asked me about a hand I played where I'd made a thin value-bet on a scary river board with just an overpair. He asked me why I'd done that and not been concerned about getting raised. Going against my better judgment, I'd told him that my opponent had called quickly on the turn, making me confident he was on the weaker side of his range and making me more comfortable going for some thin value on the river.

So cut to a few weeks later, and I'm in a hand with that good player I'd been talking to. I raise to $25 with K♥ K♣ and he calls behind me. Another player calls in the BB.

On a flop of T♠ 5♣ 3♥, I bet $40 into $75 and the good player snap calls behind me. The other player folds.

I'm immediately wary, because a snap call is unusual behavior for this player, and I'm fully aware that I was just telling him how I thought snap calls were generally weak hands. I think there's a somewhat decent chance that he flopped a set and he's trying to "level" me with a reverse tell.

The turn is the 2♥. I bet $80 into $155 and he again snap calls.

The river board is T♠ 5♣ 3♥ 2♥ 9♦.

I bet $180 into $315. While I'm concerned, I also think it's possible the tell is just a normal, run-of-the-mill tell. False tells are actually fairly rare, and being worried about "monsters under the bed" isn't the best way to play.

My opponent thinks a long time, and finally pushes out a raise to $500. I fold.

I don't know what he had, but I think it's probable he had a set and was trying to exploit me with the information I'd shared. Regardless of what he had, I think this story is a good illustration of why it does you no good to discuss reads with regular opponents. It creates confusing situations where you have to take into account past conversations. These extra factors can make it harder to know what the best action is.

River Tells

Because the stakes are higher on the river, most players will be mentally focused and stoic. Players are more likely to be thinking about ways to win the pot, with both weak and strong hands. There are fewer small clues related to not paying attention or not caring enough to conceal interest or disinterest in the hand.

Hand strength is much more defined on the river than on earlier streets. Because of this, it becomes more likely a player's emotional state will be polarized between being relaxed and being anxious, which can make these kinds of reads more possible.

Bettors will generally be stoic on the river with both weak and strong hands. Sometimes, though, bettors with strong hands will act in relaxed ways, due to already being assured of a decent pot and there being not much left to think about. For these reasons, most reliable reads you get from river bettors will be tells of relaxation. Weak-hand reads will be uncommon.

Players with weak hands will sometimes display tells of defensiveness, aimed at discouraging an opponent's bet. This is where weak-hand reads will mostly come from on the river.

Because players are mostly stoic on the river, and because the stakes are higher, player-specific reads are more important. You should usually have a sense of a player's past tendencies before using their behavior to make a big call, big fold, or big bluff.

Hand #99: Bet hesitation is sign of strength

$20-40 LHE cash game

This hand is from a limit game. The river board is 4♦ 4♣ 4♥ 8♣ J♦.

I check. My opponent, who was the pre-flop raiser and who had bet the whole way, starts to assemble a bet. He puts his chips together very slowly, with a lot of stalling movements, grabbing them from different piles, and even putting some white $1 chips into the mix.

I have 7♣ 7♥ and was planning on calling him up until that point, but his loose, relaxed behavior on the river makes it likely he has me beat: either he'd been betting a higher pair the whole time, or he'd hit the Jack.

I fold and he shows J♣ T♠.

These kinds of loose, leisurely behaviors from bettors are generally reliable tells of strength on the river. When most players bluff, they just bet normally. Bluffers have an incentive to communicate confidence and certainty. Bluffers don't want to accidentally portray indecision by having hesitations and pauses in their bets. More importantly: they don't want to be studied by an opponent for that long a time.

While the pattern holds true for most bets, it becomes more reliable on the river. On the flop or the turn, hand strength is often so undefined that you'll sometimes see people have fairly loose and prolonged behaviors even when betting weak hands. But on the river, this changes. Players bluffing on the river know they're bluffing, and know this is their last chance to win the pot. This makes their behavior more normal and straightforward overall.

But players betting strong hands will sometimes feel relaxed enough to do unusual things.

In this hand, the behavior was especially unusual, because it was a fixed limit game. Because most bets happen within a few seconds in a limit game, this makes such hesitation even more strange and likely to be a strong hand. For a lot of the more predictable fixed limit players, these kinds of small clues can help you in making folds on the river that it'd otherwise be hard to make. (This is assuming you've watched a player for a bit and ensured his hesitation before betting isn't a player-specific tell of weakness.)

To sum up: unusually hesitative or physically loose betting behaviors are generally reliable as tells of strength before the river, but on the river they become much more reliable due to large bets being mainly polarized between strong hands and bluffs.

Hand #100: Bet-motion read on regular opponent
$15-30 limit Hold'em cash game

This is an observation from a $15-30 fixed limit game.

A player I regularly played with over a few months was an unpredictable maniac, capable of all sorts of silliness. He loved to brag about how people couldn't put him on a hand. And he loved being tricky. He would do stuff like pretend to put out a raise but not follow through, or act like he was going to call to try to get a read.

This player was full of little tics and strange behaviors, and it took me a while to find something useful on him. One major thing I found was this: because this player would often abort a bluff on the turn or river when he saw that his opponent was calling, it was possible to get information from how he would move his bet into place.

For example, if he were bluffing the river, he would often take a few seconds to gather his bet and then make a wide semi-circle with his arm before placing his chips into the pot, almost like he was throwing a slow side-arm pitch. He was smart enough to realize that a lot of limit players will make their intended calls obvious, and in some cases might beat him into the pot. So if and when he saw a sign of an impending call, he was capable of aborting his bluff and giving up. However, if he saw no sign of an impending call, he would continue with his bet.

Conversely, if he were betting a decent hand, he would just put the bet out straightforwardly and quickly. No side-arm action; just a straight pushing in of the chips.

This is basically the opposite of the more typical pattern talked about in the last hand. *Again, this emphasizes how important player-specific reads are.*

With a tell like this, the interesting question becomes what to do with it. Your first instinct when noticing behavior like this might be to think something like: "When he does his slow bet thing and I have a strong hand, I'm going to act like I'm folding to encourage him to follow through with his bluff," or "When he does the slow bet when I'm weak, I'm going to act like I'm calling to discourage him from betting so I can get a free showdown, or raise him."

But neither of these is a great idea. They might work in one or two hands, but it's likely to make him notice that his behavior isn't working, which will cause him to adjust. The best approach is probably to just look stoic and not give him any sign that you're calling or folding in the hopes that he'll continue giving you some extra information.

Jonathan Little gets a bet-placement read

This next hand history comes from Jonathan Little, who's been a professional poker player since 2004 and has over $6,400,000 in live tournament cashes. He's the author of more than ten poker books, including *Excelling at No-Limit Hold'em*. He has a blog and podcast at JonathanLittlePoker.com.

This hand is from 2014. That summer in Las Vegas, when the WSOP was going on, Jonathan and I and a few others partnered to put on some poker seminars. I did a 3-hour presentation on poker tells, which included analysis of WSOP footage. Jonathan wrote the following not long after those seminars:

> The next day, I was set to play a $1,500 WSOP event. While all tournaments are important to me, in the grand scheme of things, a $1,500 event isn't too relevant. I decided to approach that tournament with one goal in mind. I was going to find and exploit a physical tell.
>
> The first part of my problem of having a difficult time finding tells is that I have constantly struggled with actively paying attention at the poker table. I have no problem following the action but quite often, I will "wake up" at the end of a hand and have no clue what happened. Other times, I will watch a person without actively quantifying in my head what I am seeing. This also leads to poor results. I have found that when I vocalize in my head what I am seeing at

the table, I both spot more d[...]
physical mannerisms and I remem[...]

There were a couple good players[...]
of these players, who I knew to be fairl[...]
sive from playing with him in the past, I not[...]
threw out his bets so that his chips were laid ou[...]
in front of him. In other words, he put them out[...]
arm fashion so they went from left to right in front o[...]

After an hour of play, I noticed he threw out his chips[...]
very different way: in a line pointing away from him.

While I wasn't sure what the difference meant, I thought it
likely meant something. A little while later, his chips went in
the pot again in the second pattern (away from himself), and
he showed up with AA. This led me to believe that that betting
motion was likely an indicator of a premium hand. I decided to
test this out by reraising him as soon as he put out the first bet
placement pattern, which happened an orbit later. His snap-
fold to my reraise provided me infinite giddiness.

Over the next few hours, I witnessed him display this
same bet placement pattern over and over. Finally, when everyone got short-stacked, which is guaranteed to happen in
fast-structured small buy-in WSOP events, a loose, aggressive kid raised to 2 big blinds from middle position and the
guy with the chip-placement tell reraised in the strong-hand
pattern to 5 big blinds from middle position.

I looked down at my cards and found the beautiful
A♥ Q♥, which is normally a premium hand, given I only had
15 big blinds. Without much thought, my A♥ Q♥ quickly
found a home in the muck pile. Luckily my read was justified when both players got all-in and the player with the
bet-placement tell had KK.

Q♣ and the river

is a stranger to

s earlier.

study me. He

ck at me again.

kes a pot-sized

an opponent

by a bet will make strong hands

 much more likely. The reason being: if a player is thinking about bluffing and wants to study an opponent, they don't want to make that studying obvious. They don't want their opponent to think: "Oh, he's studying me now. Maybe he's trying to see if I seem nervous so he can bluff." If a player is thinking about bluffing and wants to study an opponent, they will generally do so fairly surreptitiously.

I had been planning on calling, but this player's behavior got me to fold. It's generally reliable enough that I don't mind making a cold read with it in borderline situations.

Note that this is a different situation than the stack-studying behavior we talked about in Hand #63. The behavior itself is similar but the situation is very different. In Hand #63, the behavior was early in the hand and the pot was still small, and in that situation players with strong hands are mentally focused and more stoic, and also intent on not discouraging action.

On the river, when the pot is big, this tendency in many

ways reverses itself, because players making big bluffs will
be tense and will generally not want to attract attention.
And this is especially the case for this behavior, because it
can theoretically be interpreted as, "I'm studying you for
weakness and thinking about bluffing."

Hand #102: Studying opponent before call can help with later reads

$2-5 NLHE cash game

I make it $25 with J♣ J♦ in early position. I get one
caller on the button: a new player I know nothing about.

The flop is 7♦ 5♦ 4♠. I bet $35 into $57 and he calls.

The turn is the Q♥. I check and he checks quickly behind me.

The river is the T♠. I check and he bets $85 into $127.

This is a spot where I know I'm calling but I think there
can be value in waiting a few seconds and observing an
opponent before calling. *It's a chance to observe a player's
behavior when you know you'll get to see their hand.* You
might notice something that may be useful later on. It's a
chance to build a read.

In this case, this player is very still. He's staring at the
center of the table and as I stare across the table at him,
he makes no glance towards me. His eyes are wide open
and he barely blinks.

I call and he shows A♥ K♦, for ace-high.

One instance of behavior is not important. But it's a
piece of the puzzle. If I later see this player be more physically loose when betting a strong hand, I can start to form
a theory that this player's movements and stillness might
be a clue to his relaxation level.

Hand #103: Player checks river, shuffles cards

$5-10 NLHE cash game

It's the river in a 3-way pot. I was the pre-flop raiser, I bet the flop, and we all checked the turn.

The river board is: 8♣ 7♥ 2♣ 5♠ Q♥. I have J♠ T♠. Both players check to me.

When the second player checks the river, he starts shuffling his cards in an agitated way. This is a generally reliable tell of someone who's mentally checked out and is just waiting to fold. It fits someone who was calling on the flop with a club draw or a hand like T-9 and missed everything. If he had a decent pair, or better, he'd probably be a bit more focused on the situation.

These kinds of tells are much more common in multi-way pots because players aren't as competitive as they would be in heads-up pots, and so don't mind giving away their lack of interest or acting agitated.

The main caveat with this behavior is that some players shuffle their cards in lots of spots. But you'll be able to quickly take note of the players who frequently do that.

Without this extra bit of info, I wouldn't be betting this river, as I think I'll often be called by hands like 99 or A8. But knowing one player is likely to be folding I'm encouraged to bluff. *It also helps that the first player is less likely to call because he has to worry about the player behind him.*

I bet $250 into $350 and both players fold.

Hand #104: Bettor's loose behavior and smiling strengthen range
$1-2 NLHE cash game

It's a 5-way limped pot. I have T♠ 4♣ in the big blind. The flop is J♥ T♣ 5♠ and it's checked around.

The turn is the 4♦, giving me two-pair. I bet $7 into $10. A loose, weird player makes it $14. Another player calls the $14. I make it $45. Both players call.

The river is the 7♦. I check and the turn raiser checks. The last player shoves his remaining $55 into the $145. After betting, I study the player. He smiles in a very genuine, emphatic way and then puts his head down on the table in a comical way, as if hiding from me.

While I was getting a good price on calling, I thought this player's loose, relaxed behavior made a strong hand very likely. Also, 9-8 was a fairly likely hand for him to have. Also, he mostly seemed a pretty tight, by-the-book player.

I fold and the other player calls with Q♣ Q♠. The river bettor had 6♦ 3♦, for the straight.

Sometimes a few factors can combine to make it possible to fold a strong hand, even for a small bet.

Genuine smile at the 2013 WSOP ME final table

One of my most confident during-hand reads from a televised event happened in the 2013 WSOP Main Event. That year, I was consulting for final table player Amir Lehavot. Amir was eliminated in third place, and the next day I continued watching the heads-up match between Jay Farber and Ryan Riess.

The game was live with a 15-minute delay. The players' hole cards were only shown after the hand was over. (This, to me, is a fun and interesting way to watch poker. For one, your thoughts on the hand are not influenced by seeing the hole cards. And if you have an interest in poker tells, it gives you a chance to practice your reads. Unfortunately, this format is increasingly rare, because it's recognized that a mainstream audience enjoys seeing the hole cards.)

A couple hours into the heads-up match, this key hand occurred:

Jay Farber raises to 2.5M. Riess calls.

The flop is K♣ 3♠ 2♣. Riess checks. Farber bets 2.8M into 5.4M. Riess calls.

The turn is the 9♦. Riess checks. Farber bets 6M into 11M. Riess calls.

The river is the 3♣. The board is K♣ 3♠ 2♣ 9♦ 3♣.

Riess checks. Farber bets 13M into 23M.

Riess tanked for quite a while here. During that time, Farber's rail started cheering and making funny comments, and this led Farber to show a very genuine smile. At one point, it almost looked like Farber was ready to burst into laughter: that's how loose and genuine it appeared.

At that point, seeing Farber's very genuine, loose smile, I was 99% certain Farber had a strong hand. It was the most sure I'd been of any behavior I'd seen at that year's final table. It's just so hard for a bluffer to be able to fake such exuberance and enjoyment.

I was so certain, I went on Twitter at that moment and posted: "If Jay is bluffing here, I'll eat my hat. No way."

Riess ended up making a daring call with Q♠ J♣, just Queen-high. Farber had 9♣ 7♣ for the flush.

Given my certainty about this hand strength, it was kind of funny that right at that moment Norman Chad, the WSOP commentator, decided to give me a shout-out in the broadcast. After this hand was over, he quoted from a section in my book *Reading Poker Tells* where I discuss "small, arrogant smiles" from bluffers. In the book, I talk about how some bluffers can have an instinct to appear happy or relaxed and this can manifest as a small smile.

But that is a much different behavior (and one that ideally should be noticed to be player-specific before being acted on) than a player who makes a very exuberant, dynamic smile (which will be a very reliable tell, regardless of past player behavior). *While it's easy for someone who's value-betting to have a wide range of behaviors (including big smiles, small smiles, or no smiles at all), it's very hard for a bluffer, who's anxious, to have a very broad, genuine smile.*

Here are some characteristics of genuine and superficial smiles and how they differ:

- Real smiles are more likely to involve the eyes, often wrinkling the skin on the outside edges of the eyes. In contrast, fake smiles only involve the mouth.

- Real smiles are more *dynamic*, meaning they don't only remain still; they may move and change over time. Superficial smiles are often static and appear "pasted on."

- Real smiles will almost always be symmetrical, involving both sides of the mouth. Fake smiles will sometimes involve only one side of the mouth.

It's worth comparing this hand where Farber smiled genuinely to a hand a bit earlier in the match where Farber made a similar triple-barrel bet, was bluffing, and also smiled a bit.

The hand begins with Riess raising pre-flop and Farber calling.

The flop is 3♠ 3♥ 7♣.

Farber checks. Riess bets and Farber calls.

The turn is 2♣. Farber checks. Riess bets 5M and Farber check-raises to 13.45M. Riess calls.

The river is the 9♠. The board is 3♠ 3♥ 7♣ 2♣ 9♠.

Farber bets 24.5M into a pot of 38.2M. After a good wait, someone on the rail shouts out, "You gotta pay to see these cards, son!" Riess looks at Farber, trying to interact with him visually. Farber wears a small, slight smile on his face for a minute or so as Riess thinks.

In the moment, this smile did not tell me much and I didn't have much opinion about it. When it comes to more subtle smiles—and behaviors in general—you'll find that players with both strong hands and weak hands are easily capable of that behavior. This is also harder to read because Farber's behavior was caused by something external. When external events induce behavior, it can be harder to judge what it means. (Although if his smile was as genuine-seeming and dynamic as the smile in the other hand, it wouldn't matter what caused it.)

Riess ended up folding Q♥ 7♠ here; a pair of 7s. Farber was bluffing, with 6♦ 5♥.

This comparison helps explain why strong-hand reads of bettors are so much easier to make than are weak-hand reads. *Strong hand reads usually happen when you read a bettor for being very relaxed and doing something it'd be unlikely for them to do if they were bluffing.* Whereas with subtle behaviors, which most big-bet behaviors are, they're easily capable of being displayed with both strong hands and weak hands.

Hand #105: Shrug-like gesture when betting strengthens range
$2-5 PLO cash game

This is a Pot-Limit Omaha hand from the Chicago-based Windy City Championships televised cash games. I used this hand in my poker tells video series.

We'll go straight to the river:

The river board is A♥ K♣ 3♣ Q♠ 7♥ and it's heads-up. The pot is $1,200.

The first player checks and the second player announces all-in for about $700. As he does this, he makes a quick but subtle palms-up gesture with his hand.

A shrug can have multiple parts:

- A lift of the shoulders
- A palms-up movement of the hand or hands
- A head tilt

Put all of these together and you have a stereotypical, obvious shrug. But more subtle shrugging gestures might only include one or two of these elements.

In this hand, the bettor had only a quick, subtle palms-up gesture but it still has the general meaning of a shrug, which communicates, "I don't really care" or, "It doesn't matter." You could think of a shrug as a physical weak-hand statement, implying something like: "This situation doesn't matter. I could be shoving with a wide range here because it's not an important situation. You shouldn't take it that seriously, either."

In this hand, the player had K♣ J♦ J♥ T♥, for a straight, the nuts.

Shrugs from bettors are generally going to indicate strength and relaxation.

But there are a few reasons it can be difficult to interpret this kind of behavior as strong-hand behavior:

- Bluffers can also have a motivation to communicate indifference. Bluffers might shrug due to an unconscious desire to communicate, "It doesn't matter to me if I shove or if you call because I've got a strong hand and I'm relaxed either way." Because shrugs communicate indifference, it muddies the waters. A tell that means 'I don't care' is different and more ambiguous than a tell that communicates 'I'm unhappy with the situation.' Behaviors expressing unhappiness and concern are more meaningful tells than behaviors expressing ambivalence.

- Bluffers and players betting weak hands are capable of shrugging due to being agitated. Sometimes anxious bettors do unusual things because it's a method of alleviating their anxiety. This is true for a good amount of ostentatious behavior from bettors, which can sometimes make it difficult to differentiate agitation and anxiety from relaxed behavior (and this is another reason player-specific correlation is so important). One example of how this might play out: a player four-bet shoves all-in with 8♠ 7♠ and as his opponent stares at him, he makes an exaggerated shrug. This player feels nervous about the situation and doesn't enjoy his opponent studying him, and he has an instinct to move around and show he's relaxed. Related to the point above, it might make sense that this player selects a behavior that communicates, "Do whatever you want; I don't care either way."

- Players with short stacks can easily have some honest ambivalence and shrugging behaviors when shoving pre-flop with weak hands. Because there is less at stake than if they had a larger stack, the situation may actually not matter that much to them.

Having said all that, shrugging gestures from bettors generally will indicate strong hands. This becomes more true on later streets, when:

- Hand strength is more defined and bets are more likely to indicate polarized hand strengths.
- Players making big bluffs will be mostly stoic and inconspicuous.

To put some of these ideas in context: in the PLO hand just described, where the player shoves the river with a slight palms-up gesture, I'd feel confident that this big-bet behavior on the river was likely to indicate strength, whereas if it had been a pre-flop shove, I think it could easily be a wide range of hands.

One final note about this hand: this player's slight palms-up shrug was subtle and small, not exaggerated.

This increases the chances it fits the general pattern and indicates relaxation and a strong hand. *In general, subtle behaviors are more reliable than exaggerated behaviors when it comes to the common weak-behavior-means-strong-hand and strong-behavior-means-weak-hand tells.* The more exaggerated a bet-related behavior is, the more likely it becomes that:

- The player is doing it due to some agitation resulting from the stress of bluffing.

- The player is doing it consciously, as a reverse tell.

Hand #106: Shrug after question about chip stack
$2-5 NLHE cash game

It's heads-up. The river board is Q♣ Q♠ T♠ 5♥ 6♠. I have K♦ Q♥.

My opponent bets $255 into the $400 pot.

I can't see my opponent's chip stack and I'm curious how much he left himself behind. I ask him how much he has. He lifts up his arms and makes a shrugging, palms-up gesture with his hands, referring to his chips.

Unlike shrug-like gestures associated with bets, shrugging in response to someone asking about the chip stack is not likely to contain meaning. It's common to see players respond with shrug-like gestures when someone asks for a chip count, whether they have a strong hand or a weak hand. *This is understandable because the behavior is induced by a specific question, and in context the shrugging behavior has a specific and understood meaning of, "I'm not sure what my stack is exactly."*

In this hand, the player's shrugging gesture has no

effect on my decision and I end up calling.

I mention this hand to emphasize that the shrugging behavior referenced in the last hand history is only meaningful when associated with a bet or raise. As with many behaviors, the context in which a behavior occurs is very important. *A major mistake players make when trying to read tells is thinking that a behavior in one situation will mean the same thing in another situation.*

Hand #107: Regular opponent agitated when betting weak hand
$2-5 NLHE cash game

The next few hands all feature the same opponent: I'll call him Joey. I've played with Joey a good amount over the last few years at $2-5 and $5-10. I've got a fairly reliable tell on him: when he makes a big bet and has agitated, quick movements, he's likely to be weak. When he makes a big bet and acts in a casual, "smoother" manner, he's more likely to have a strong hand. I'll show a few hands where this tell influenced my decisions. (Not all of these focus on river situations but I thought it best to group these hand histories together.)

In this hand, both Joey and I have about $1,000 to start the hand. I have 2♠ 2♣ and raise to $15 UTG. Joey makes it $40 in middle position and I call.

The flop is T♥ 5♥ 2♥. I check and Joey bets $60 into the $87 pot with a good amount of forward force. He also seems somewhat agitated; he's moving around with a lot of quick movements and he's sneaking glances at me. His agitation makes me confident he didn't flop a set or a flush. It doesn't rule out all strong hands; *it just makes the strongest hands less likely*. With those hands, from my experience playing with him, I think he'd be more thoughtful and smooth in his actions.

I make it $200. Joey shoves within a few seconds and I call. He has A♥ A♣.

Without having this read on this player, I would have to play this hand much more cautiously, because I'd usually only be getting significant action on the flop from a higher set or a flush. AA with a heart is one of the few hands that I beat and that he'd be willing to get all-in on the flop with.

Hand #108: Another agitation-when-betting read of weakness

$2-5 NLHE cash game

There are two limps, including Joey. I make it $25 in late position with 8♣ 7♣. Joey calls me in early position.

The flop is 7♦ 6♥ 6♦. Joey checks. I bet $40 into $62 and he calls.

The turn is the 6♣. I bet $65 into $142. Joey check-raises to $130 quickly. I call. I do not think he'd snap-min-raise with quad 6s, although it's possible. I think an overpair is unlikely.

The river is the K♠. He fairly quickly bets $300 into $402.

This was obviously a bad card, as he could have had a flush draw with a King. And of course he could have the 6 and have played it a bit strangely to confuse me.

Joey looks agitated; he looks around the room with a lot

of small movements, and doesn't look at me.

I ask him, "You got a six?" He doesn't answer, but after a few seconds, he stands up and looks down at the board, with his arms crossed. I was on the fence about it, leaning towards calling, but his agitated behavior made it that much easier. I called: he had T♠ 7♠ and we split the pot.

I want to emphasize that this is a *player-specific read*. In general, standing after making a big bet is a pretty reliable tell of relaxation. If I saw a stranger act this way when making a big bet, my cold read would be that he was likely relaxed and strong. But in this case, I've been able to form a long-term, more-tailored read for this player.

Hand #109: Agitated raise weakens range

$5-10 NLHE cash game

Joey raises in late position, first in, to $35. I'm in the small blind with A♠ K♥ and make it $115. He calls.

The flop is T♦ 8♣ 2♠. I check and Joey checks behind.

The turn is the 8♦, putting two diamonds out. I bet $100 into $235. Joey immediately raises to $280, with a lot of movement. I call.

The river is a 2♥. I check. He quickly bets $500 into $795. Again, he seems very agitated, moving his head around with quick movements.

I call. He shows A♦ 5♦: we split the pot.

I wouldn't have called the river here if it wasn't for his agitation and speed of betting. And again, it's only because I'm familiar with his behavior. Also a factor: there were a good amount of diamond draws I could see him playing this way.

Hand #110: A second-hand read

$2-5 NLHE cash game

The river board is T♥ 7♥ 2♥ K♠ 2♣. My opponent bets $300 into $500. I have A♥ A♣ and I'm on the fence.

I ask my opponent, "Will you show?"

"If you call," he says. "If you call, I'll show." He's stating the obvious (that he would have to show his hand if I called) in a joking way. It doesn't tell me anything; I could imagine him saying this with both strong and weak hands.

Then he picks his cards up off the table and shows them to the two guys beside him (one of whom is Joey from the last few hands). The three of them are all friendly with each other; I think they might even hang out away from the poker table.

After I think a little more, he says, "*They* know what I have," referring to his friends beside him.

I look at the players beside him. They're both players I've played with a lot. Although we're all friendly, they're definitely on his side, and would prefer he win.

"So what does he have?" I ask them jokingly.

Neither of them is looking much at me; they're mostly looking at the board cards in the middle of the table or down directly in front of them. Knowing what I know of these guys, if their friend had a big hand, both of them would enjoy looking at me and relishing the moment a bit. Many players enjoy seeing a vanquished enemy squirm. But these guys are avoiding eye contact.

"He'll kill me if I tell you," Joey says, looking down and smiling.

These guys don't seem happy about the situation.

They're uncomfortable, and they don't want to give away information about their friend's hand, so they're trying to seem relaxed.

In a way, they're acting like bluffers themselves. Bluffers usually avoid eye contact and don't like to interact. (Some players will stare more when bluffing, but the opposite pattern is more common.)

I call and the bettor mucks.

When players show their cards to people near them, they can unintentionally spread feelings associated with bluffing or value-betting, and you might be able to pick something up from those people. You might call this a "second-hand" read.

Also worth noting: depending on the cardroom rules and how strictly they're enforced, it might not be allowed to question the other players like I did here. Where this hand took place, the atmosphere was quite informal, and I knew it was unlikely anyone would be upset by my questions.

Hand #111: The high-hand board read
$2-5 NLHE cash game

This hand was sent to me from Jake Farrow, a poker player in Maryland. He talks about a pretty rare tell. But it's a fun one, and it also shows the importance of always paying attention and giving a decision a little thought before acting:

> I've got $650 in this $2-5 game. A player in middle position opens for $20. There's one caller. Hero has A♠ K♦ on the button and makes it $75.

SB folds. BB looks at me, shuffles chips, looks at me, shuffles chips. He tanks for about 20 seconds and calls. Other players fold. Pot is around $200.

Flop comes A♥ Q♠ 7♣. SB checks. I bet $85, he calls. Pot is around $350.

Turn is a Q♣. He checks, I check.

River is another Ace, the A♣. He sits for a while, and says, "Hold on, fellas. Let me think about this for a bit."

At that point, he makes an obvious glance towards the high-hand TV display, which shows a straight flush as the current high hand. The clock only has 1 minute 20 seconds left before the next high-hand time period starts.

The Villain waits until that clock runs out, then he goes all-in for his remaining $550 into the $350 pot.

My thinking is that either this is the sickest act ever—either with a pure bluff, or with an Ace to get me off the chopped pot—or he has QQ for quads. Supporting evidence that he has QQ:

His glance at the high-hand board.

His waiting for the new high-hand period to start.

But would he really be that obvious about it if he had QQ? Am I being leveled?

I've got a little doubt, but mostly I'm thinking it would be way too complex and weird an act to do with a bluff or an Ace. Most players at low stakes aren't anywhere near that creative or ballsy.

I'm getting like 1.4:1 on a call and I don't like to fold the very top of my range. But I just don't see any way that he doesn't have QQ. He raised pre and tanked like 20 seconds before calling my three-bet: I think he was thinking about four-betting me there.

I say, "This is so sick. You've got Queens, don't you?"

He doesn't say anything. I say, "Let me see a Queen, so I can fold." Then I show my hand.

He says, "You're gonna fold that?"

I say, "I'm thinking about it. Let me see a Queen and I'll fold."

He says, "Nah, man. You wanna see the hand, you gotta pay."

This behavior is kind of hostile and goading, and that's another piece of evidence that he wants me to call.

I say, "Well, I'll know soon enough anyway because you'll be on the high-hand board, right?" He just nods, seeming very relaxed.

I fold and the table starts berating me. He flips over Q♦ Q♥ for the quads.

Thoughts from Zach: Worth mentioning: this behavior and read would depend on house rules. In some cardrooms, to be eligible for the high hand prize, the hand must go to showdown, which would make this behavior unlikely, as the bettor wouldn't want his opponent to fold. Also, in some rooms, the high-hand clock would be based on when the hand started, not when it ended.

I had a similar read on an opponent years ago. It was at a $20-40 limit game, where a player made a subtle glance at the high-hand board before betting the river, and that convinced me to fold a hand I was planning on calling with. And I've talked to a couple other players who have had similar experiences. So it's possible you'll one day see it.

I wanted to mention a bet-sizing pattern in this hand. When a recreational player chooses a bet size that's a lot larger than you think they would size a bluff, it's very likely that it's a value-bet. Most recreational players won't choose a very large bet size when bluffing. *Your average recreational player will choose the lowest amount he thinks will do the job.* He doesn't want to bluff big because, so he thinks, he's either getting called or he's not, so a bigger bet is just wasting money if he's called.

In a typical river-bluffing scenario, a recreational player will choose a ½-pot or ¾-pot-sized bet. A pot-sized bet or higher will make it more likely the player is relaxed and going for value. (And keep in mind I'm talking about recreational players who haven't shown evidence of being capable of making big bluffs. Obviously once you see a player capable of big bluffs, you'll take that into account.)

When you're on the fence about calling or folding to an opponent's bet, ask yourself, "Would this player, from what I've seen of him, choose this bet sizing if he were bluffing? What's the most likely sizing this player would have used if he were going to bluff here?"

Hand #112: Unusually large bet-sizing
$2-5 NLHE cash game

This is another example of the bet-sizing tell talked about in the last hand history. (It's from the flop, but I thought this was a good spot for it.)

A player limps UTG. This player is weird: he's done several illogical things in the few hours I've played with him. He's capable of weird, aggressive bets and also capable of being very nitty.

Another player limps and a late position player raises to

$30. The UTG limper is the only caller.

The flop is A♣ K♠ T♦. The UTG limper fairly quickly shoves $400 into the $70 pot.

What hands would he be likely to do this with? Almost immediately I thought a set was the most likely hand, for a few reasons:

- I don't think he'd do this with the straight. It's a rare player who wants to scare off action with a hand that's so dominant.

- I think he almost always has to have something very strong to do this.

- I think with two-pair he doesn't like the situation facing a pre-flop raiser. He'd hate to make this bet with two-pair and be snap-called by AK or a set. Same with single-pair hands.

The same bet-sizing pattern from the last hand history applies here: if this player were going to choose to bluff here, he could obviously choose a much lower amount. The abnormally high bet-size makes it likely he's relaxed and has some sort of very strong hand. At the same time, I think he's unlikely to want to scare away action with a straight. So sets are the only very strong hand left. Besides the most likely set of TT, I think his UTG limp and call still leave KK and AA in his range, especially as he has shown himself to be a strange player.

The 3-straight board would also be a potential factor in his doing something weird like this with a set. For a lot of recreational players in this situation, a Jack or a Ten on the turn will make them hate life. This is the case for a lot of overbets from recreational players with strong hands;

they don't want to face a tough decision. *They'd rather potentially scare away action with an overly large bet than take a chance of facing a tough decision later in the hand.*

It's also easy to imagine that this player would think there was at least a decent chance his shove would get called, because the pre-flop raiser could easily have AK or AQ.

His opponent does end up calling the shove with A♠ Q♠. The UTG player shows A♥ A♦, for a set.

JAMIE KERSTETTER
on poker tells

Jamie Kerstetter has been playing poker for a living since 2009, both online and live, with a focus on tournaments. This is from a talk we had in 2014.

ELWOOD: Do you have any good stories about poker tells or behavior?

KERSTETTER: I had one recently. This was from a $500 WSOP circuit event. I'm not someone who ever really tanks that long, ever. But I was so glad I did it in this one hand. We only had a few tables left and were approaching the money. Me and the villain both had around 80 big blinds and the rest of the table had around 25 big blinds. And most people in this kind of situation don't make it a point to get involved in big pots with the other big chip stack. He didn't seem good; just a random guy.

Long story short, he made a huge overbet on the river,

shoving all in for about a pot-and-a-half sized bet. I had a pair, just a bluff-catcher, but his line didn't make sense. The way the hand played out, I was expecting him to either bet small for value or check and let me bluff with my missed draws. But the river came and he just shoved. I was leaning toward folding but it was definitely a borderline spot that required some thought. And during the whole time I'm thinking he seems pretty comfortable but he's not moving much, just mostly still.

After about three minutes I'm getting ready to muck my hand. And a friend of mine comes over to the table and says something about going to Argentina and my opponent unfreezes and says, "Oh, you're from Argentina? I lived in Argentina," attempting a relaxed conversation in a very tense moment. It wasn't until he broke his pose and started talking that I realized how uncomfortable he had been sitting still for so long. It seemed suddenly really obvious to me and I called right away after that. He was bluffing.

ELWOOD: How have your thoughts on the importance of poker behavior changed over the years, as you've played more?

KERSTETTER: I used to think they were way more important than they actually are because I used to play with very bad players who just weren't aware of what they were doing — and they were giving away a lot of free information to anyone paying attention. As you move up in levels, you play with more good players, so tells become less relevant. When you're playing pretty high, you're up against a lot of very stoic players who have been through it all and don't give off much because they're not really affected all that much by specific poker hands anymore.

But when you're playing against bad players, it's worth it to watch their every move. You get some real tell-boxes. I was playing in this New York club recently. It was satisfying because this one really mean guy had a pretty reliable tell. Whenever he was betting weak, he would almost always verbalize his bets. For example, he'd bluff the river and say, "Three twenty five" in a really confident voice. And then when he was strong, he'd be quiet as a mouse. Hero-calling this man was fun because he'd get so enraged and berate me for calling with such weak holdings, not ever knowing he was the one making it possible.

Mainly, though, I think tells are useful for close decisions. Like, I'm not going to make a big decision and just snap call someone based only on a tell unless the player has proven again and again that the tell is reliable. But if I'm undecided either way and I think I've got something that's a little poker tell on someone, then I'll be moved in that direction.

Hand #113: A bet announcement read

$25,000 buy-in WPT NLHE tournament

Dutch Boyd has been playing poker professionally since before 2000. At the time of writing this, he has three WSOP bracelets and has made eight WSOP final tables. He also has a popular Twitch stream. You can check out his website at DutchBoyd.com.

In this hand, he recounts a situation from back in the

day where some prior player-specific analysis paid off:

> If you've been following poker since before the Money-
> maker boom started in 2003, you probably remember Paul
> Phillips. Paul was a well-known player on the live tourna-
> ment circuit who'd achieved considerable success in the
> early days of televised poker. He was an imaginative, cre-
> ative player who it was said had cashed out for millions in a
> dot-com startup.
>
> Maybe it was the fearlessness that resulted from not need-
> ing a big tournament score to pay the bills, but Paul was
> always willing to risk a big bluff if he smelled weakness and
> felt like he could get an opponent off a hand. He crushed
> the tournament circuit back in 2003 and 2004, having one
> of the best years in the poker history books. He won a WPT
> title, had a WPT runner-up finish, and made four WSOP
> final tables.
>
> I got to play with Paul in one of my very first WPT main
> events. It's been more than a decade now, so the memory is
> a little shaky as to the time and place. But I'm fairly sure it
> was during Day 1 of the 2004 Bellagio WPT Champion-
> ship. This was a $25,000 buy-in event and the biggest tour-
> nament I'd played at that point in my life. It no doubt would
> have been an intimidating day for me under normal circum-
> stances. Having Philips directly to my right didn't help my
> comfort level.
>
> If memory serves, we started the day with 50,000 tourna-
> ment chips. Paul hit the ground running, playing very ag-
> gressively and showing a willingness to enter a lot of pots.
> He also seemed to have a knack of always having it when he
> reached a showdown. After a few hours of play, the antes

kicked in and Paul got even more aggressive.

I believe we were at 200/400 blinds with a 50 ante. Paul made a raise in the hijack to 1,200. I looked down in the cut-off at 9♠ 9♣, and decided to just flat call. Both blinds folded.

The flop was K♣ 6♥ 5♥.

"Bet." Paul announced his action in a low, hollow, monotone voice with a downward inflection. He counted out chips and fired out a bet of around 2,000.

Under normal circumstances, this would not have been a great way to start a hand.

But let's rewind a few months.

Do you remember when I told you Paul had a WPT runner-up finish? It had been during the 2003 Legends of Poker tournament at the Bicycle Casino. He finished second to Mel Judah, winning almost $300,000. The rest of the final table was full of ringers—T.J. Cloutier came in 3rd, Chip Jett got 4th, Farzad Bonyadi came in 5th. And in 6th place was one of my best poker buds at the time, Phil Laak.

Back then, I looked up a lot to Phil. That was one reason I spent more than eight hours on a weekday watching that footage when it aired. Armed with a notebook, I studied the tape like a football coach might study a rival team before a bowl game. Laak busted out fairly quickly, but after an hour of using the Tivo remote to pause and rewind key hands, I was pretty confident about a few behavioral leaks Laak might have had in a few hands.

Watching more, I started to become confident that I had a good read on Paul Phillips.

Hand after hand, the same thing happened:

Paul would furrow his brow.

He'd announce his bet.

He'd count chips.

He'd place them out in front of him.

And I'd pause and rewind. I started to see a major difference between how Paul acted when he was betting a strong hand versus when he was bluffing.

What really stood out to me was his vocal inflection. He'd say the same words, but the difference was night and day. A high, sing-songy feeling when he was happy with his hand. A low, hollow, downward inflection when he was on a bluff.

Back to the hand versus Phillips. My pocket nines. His low, hollow, monotone voice announcing, "Bet," on a K-6-5 board.

There was no guesswork involved. I didn't have to wonder if Paul had hit his top pair. I *knew* my pocket nines were the best hand. So I made the call, confident that Phillips would continue his aggressive line and confident that I'd be able to discern exactly where I was at in the rest of the hand.

The turn came the Q♦.

Again, Paul announced his bet. Same low, hollow tone. This time he counted out 6000 chips and slid them into the middle. I took my time, trying to feign discomfort, then made the call.

The dealer burned and the river hit the felt. It was another low heart, putting three hearts out.

Once more, Paul announced his bet in that same hollow tone. He fired out nearly a pot-sized bet.

I made the call. Quickly.

Paul turned over ace-high and I took down a huge pot with a mediocre hand. We'd put in more than half our stacks into the pot by the river. My intensive study session of that WPT final table had paid off with around $12,000 in equity.

Unfortunately, I wouldn't end up realizing that equity. A few hours later, after Paul had busted, I found myself in a big hand against an old-school player named Mo Ibrahim. I'd flopped top two pair with K-J on a K-J-T flop. Mo shoved all-in with AQ. In hindsight, he was clearly exhibiting some of the strong tells that Zach has talked about in his books and videos. (To name one thing: he got up out of his chair and stood up after shoving.)

If Zach's material was around ten years ago, maybe I'd have found the fold. But as it was, it was a tough spot. I called and that was that.

Hand #114: Re-evaluating a read

$2-5 NLHE cash game

Two players limp. I limp in the cut-off with A♣ 2♣. Another player limps on the button.

The flop is J♦ J♠ 2♠. Three players check and I bet $15 into $30. The player behind me calls immediately. An immediate call makes it less likely this player has a Jack. If he had a Jack on a two-flush flop, he'd usually want to consider the situation a little bit. It doesn't make it super-unlikely that he has a Jack; just a bit less likely.

The turn is a 3♦. I check and he bets $25 into $60. I call.

The river is the 5♥. I check. He thinks for a few seconds, double-checks his cards, then bets $60 into $110.

I debate calling, especially because I think this player

would bet more with trips or better. But the double-check of his cards influences me to fold. As discussed earlier, this is a pretty reliable tell of strength when exhibited right before a bet; a bluffer will usually just bet in a straightforward manner.

Much more importantly, I'd played with this player a good amount and had observed that he fairly often double-checked his cards before betting strong hands. Considering it's a pretty borderline call to begin with, even if this tell were only slightly reliable in the long term, it'd still be useful in this spot.

This illustrates some of the value of reading tells in no-limit games. Sometimes tells can give you a chance to re-evaluate a decision on the river, when the bets are largest. Theoretically, if you had decent reads on an opponent's behavior, you could play somewhat sub-optimally before the river, when the bets are small, and still have an edge because you'd more often be making correct decisions when the bets are big.

Hand #115: Post-bet eye-contact tells from regular opponent
$5-10 NLHE cash game

The next two hands feature the same player: we'll call him Steve. I have a pretty decent read on Steve. When he makes big bets with a strong hand, he's more likely to make eye contact and engage in other ways. When he's bluffing, he's more stoic and neutral.

In a way, it could be thought of as almost opposite of Joey's behavior discussed in earlier hands; Joey was more

calm and stoic when betting strong hands and more animated when betting weak hands. As you probably know
by now, these things can vary a good amount from person
to person, but the more we can understand the possible
patterns and the underlying reasons, the easier it gets to
recognize patterns in opponents.

In this hand, Steve limps UTG+1. Another player
makes it $50. I call in late position with 9♣ 9♠. Steve
makes what is basically a min-three-bet to $110. I'd seen
him do something similar earlier in the day with AK. The
third player calls. I call.

The flop is 7♣ 6♠ 6♥. Steve checks, the other player
checks, and I bet $120 into $345. Steve calls and the third
player folds.

This is a bit worrisome because if Steve had AK or AQ
or something similar, I believe he'd just be betting the
flop. At the same time, he's a very loose and unpredictable
player, so it's hard to pin him down too much to specific
ranges.

The turn is the J♦. He checks and I check behind.

The river comes the 3♠.

Steve quickly bets $300 into $565. He puts his hand
under his chin in a kind of submissive posture and looks
at me steadily.

Without the eye contact from him, I would have been
much more on the fence here. He's fully capable of strange
plays and reckless bluffs. *But I've played with him enough to
know that when he looks at his opponent after betting, he's relaxed and usually has it.*

I fold and he shows 6♦ 5♦, for trips.

Worth reiterating: when this player *doesn't* engage in eye contact with me, it's not nearly as meaningful as when he *does* make eye contact. This is because not making eye contact is his (and most players') standard behavior, whether with a weak or a strong hand. Not engaging in eye contact does make weak hands a bit more likely, but it's not anywhere near as meaningful compared to the eye-contact-after-betting. This reinforces the general concept of: *the absence of a tell is not necessarily a tell.*

Hand #116: Bet thrown towards opponent
$5-10 NLHE cash game

In this hand, there are two limps and I make it $60 in the small blind with K♦ Q♣. Steve calls in middle position and we're heads-up.

The flop is Q♦ 8♥ 4♦. I bet $65 into $140 and he calls.

The turn is the 6♣. I check and he bets $150 into $270. I call.

The river is the 9♥. I check and Steve bets $315 into $570. He does something unusual when he puts in the bet, though. We are sitting three seats away, both facing the dealer, and when he bets, he tosses it in a little bit closer to me than he has to. It was not in any way extreme: he just angled the bet more towards me a few inches further than would otherwise be normal.

When someone throws a bet towards you, it can be seen as a goading behavior. It can be interpreted as saying, "I dare you to call this." And goading behavior is almost always done by bettors with strong hands. Bluffers don't want to accidentally trigger your "calling reflex" (as Mike

Caro called it in his *Book of Poker Tells*). They don't want to trigger you calling out of anger or spite. Like most unusual behaviors done when making large bets, it will indicate relaxation.

In this case, there were few strong hands I could actually put him on: 9-8 was one, maybe a flush draw that turned into a straight, maybe J-T. In a vacuum I would have called, but with this small clue, I opted to fold.

I didn't find out what he had, but I'm confident enough in the behavior to feel good about the fold. This behavior also fit in with this player's general tendency to interact more with his opponents when relaxed, whether that was with his eyes or with other behaviors.

Hand #117: Immediate bet from tight player
$2-5 NLHE cash game

A very tight player makes it $20 pre-flop. I call with Q♠ J♠ on the button.

The flop is Q♦ 8♥ 6♥. He bets $25 into $47. I call.

The turn is the J♣. He bets $45 into $97. I call.

The river is the 2♥. He quickly bets $100 into $187.

We discussed bet-timing earlier, with a focus on how immediate bets skew towards bluffs. But in some situations, immediate bets make very strong hands clearly more likely. This is one such case. When a tight player makes a significant bet immediately, it will almost always be with a very strong hand. The tighter they are, the more reliable this will be. *This is mainly because tight players, for the most part, are not capable of quickly reaching a decision to bluff.* To put it another way: their quick-bluff range is almost non-existent.

If this player had an overpair or a set, the flush draw completing would make him pause a moment. If he were going to bluff, he'd likely want to consider the situation a few moments before betting. This is especially true considering he is first to act. (An immediate bet would be less reliable if he were second to act.)

Based on what I knew of his play, I thought A♥ Q♥ was almost the only hand he could have, so I folded.

Hand #118: Snap bet from decent aggro player
$5-10 NLHE cash game

An experienced and maybe too-aggressive player in late position raises to $35. I call in the BB with A♠ T♣.

The flop is T♥ 9♠ 5♣. I check and he bets $50. I call.

The turn is another 5: the 5♠. I check and he bets $140 into $175. I call.

The river is the 2♣.

After a few seconds I check and he immediately, super quickly, throws chips into the pot: $370 into $455.

Based on my knowledge of this player, this is very unlikely to be a bluff, for a few reasons:

- This player and I have history. He knows that I know that he's very aggressive and capable of making big and frequent bluffs. For this reason, he'd be unlikely to do something like this because it might make it seem like he's just desperately bombing as a bluff.

- This player is generally balanced with his bet-timing. He's fully capable of betting quickly when bluffing, but even his quick bets are typically after a second or two. This strangely quick bet here is a sign that he's relaxed and not really concerned with how his behavior is interpreted. (This boils down to the general rule of: *strange behavior from players making big bets tends to indicate strength.*)

- This player is experienced. He's not the type to feel "painted into a corner" and pressured to bluff, which will sometimes be a factor when trying to interpret immediate bets from recreational players.

- This was unusual behavior for him. I couldn't remember the last time I'd seen him bet this quickly. Because it was strange for him, he was less likely to be balanced with it.

For all of these reasons, I was confident he had a very strong hand. Even if I thought this was only a weakly reliable strong-hand tell, this would be helpful in deciding a borderline call/fold decision. I folded and he showed 5♦ 5♥ for quads.

Hand #119: Quick bets when board texture changes
2007 WSOP $10K NLHE Main Event

This next hand is from the 2007 WSOP Main Event.

The WSOP episodes are edited, so it's hard to know for certain how closely the bet-timing in this hand matches what actually happened. I've been told by a WSOP producer that they generally avoid making actions seem like snap-bets or snap-checks if there are long pauses present, so I tend to think the timing is fairly accurate. In any case, we'll just assume it's accurate for the sake of learning, as I think it's a good example of how board texture can help with a read.

On a flop of 8♥ 7♥ 3♥, the pre-flop raiser, Winston, bets 150K into a pot of 232K. His opponent, Kenny Tran, calls him with A♦ 8♠.

The turn is another heart: the 2♥. After just a few seconds, Winston announces "350," betting 350K into the 532K pot. Kenny Tran calls again.

The river pairs the board: the 2♦. Winston, after a few seconds, announces "700," betting 700K into 1.32M.

As discussed earlier, quick bets often polarize a player's range to strong and weak hands. On the turn, when Winston bets quickly, we can assume his range is probably the A♥ (maybe the K♥) or a bluff. If he had a heart weaker than the A♥, or if he had a hand weaker than a flush, he'd probably want to think a little bit about the situation. It's very unlikely he'd bet a set or two-pair so quickly on a four-flush board.

On the river, when the board pairs, his large, quick bet is also polarizing: it's likely he's either got a full-house or a bluff. And him having a full house contradicts his probable range after betting the turn. If he *did* have the A♥ or the K♥ on the turn, it's likely he'd want to think for a while before betting the river, as the board texture has changed so much and a full house is now possible.

For some quick and large bets, changes in the board texture can help you in picking out a bluff. *When the board changes dramatically and a bettor doesn't seem to be thoughtful about that change, it can be a clue that they're bluffing.*

In this hand, Kenny Tran thought about it quite a while and eventually called with his pair of 8s. Winston had A♠ T♣, for just Ace-high. Tran is an experienced live player, known for being good at reading people. It's possible the speed of his opponent's bets played a role in his decision here.

Hand #120: Pre-load of bet raises suspicion

$1,100 buy-in NLHE tournament

This next hand comes from Jonathan Levy, who's been a professional poker player since 2009. Levy and his friend Grant Denison make up *The Poker Guys*. They put out regular video analysis of televised poker hands on Youtube, talking about strategy and behavior. You can find that at YouTube.com/HandOfTheWeek. They also have a podcast, The Breakdown, available at ThePokerGuys. net.

Here's a hand Jonathan played where an opponent's behavior changed his mind:

> I was playing the $1100 Deepstacks Main Event in Oregon. I called from the BB with A♥ 4♥. There were four of us in the hand. I flopped the nut flush draw on a Q♠ T♥ 7♥ board. It checked through.
>
> The turn was the 4♠, bringing a second flush draw. The small blind bet out. I called with bottom pair and the nut flush draw.
>
> As the dealer was burning the river, the small blind began putting chips together for a bet.
>
> The river was the 8♠ and the small blind bet almost as soon as the river hit the felt. I couldn't imagine why someone would choose the amount before they knew the river card

and bet as though it didn't matter that the flush came in. I called pretty quickly with bottom pair specifically because of this fast river bet.

"I have nothing," he said and mucked his cards.

Hand #121: Immediate river bet polarizes and strengthens range

2014 Heartland Poker Tour $1650 NLHE tournament

Chris DeMaci raises in middle position with K♥ J♥. Lily Kiletto, a serious player, calls directly behind with A♠ A♣.

Three players see a flop of 2♣ 2♥ 2♠. DeMaci bets 108K into 220K. Kiletto calls.

The turn is the Q♠. DeMaci bets 210K into 438K. Kiletto calls.

The river is the 6♠. DeMaci checks quickly. Kiletto immediately announces "All in," for 521K into 858K.

This is a case where an immediate bet is likely to indicate a very strong hand. Kiletto called on the flop with a player behind and called on the turn, so her range is pretty strong there, with a lot of pairs from small to large. Immediate bets are polarized to very strong hands and bluffs and, in this case, there are no pure bluffs in her river-betting range. And because it takes time to evaluate what to do with medium-strength hands, it's unlikely she'd be betting immediately with medium-strength hands. For example, while it's possible she might turn a hand like TT into a bluff, it's very unlikely she'd do so immediately.

In this case, I think her range for immediately betting the river is almost entirely AA and QQ (and quads if she was capable of calling pre-flop with any deuce-containing hands).

This immediate river bet would make me comfortable folding many strong hands if I were her opponent. Even with KK here, I think a fold could be logically defended because of the points mentioned. This is especially the case if we think that Kiletto is capable of calling and not three-betting pre-flop with AA or QQ.

Worth noting: her opponent's quick river check is a factor here. *If he'd thought for a while before checking, her quick bet would be less meaningful, because she would have had more time to think about the situation and potentially plan turning a medium-strength hand into a bluff.*

Hand #122: Deceptive bet-timing with Jonathan Little

This next hand history comes from Jonathan Little (JonathanLittlePoker.com).

Before each heads-up Global Poker League match I play, I make a point to watch as much footage of my opponent as I can. I look for specific exploitable plays they make and also try to figure out how they approach poker. In my most recent match, it became clear that my opponent (one of the best high-stakes heads-up players in the world) places a decent amount of value on timing tells. I came to the conclusion that he thought most players acted in a somewhat obvious manner, playing quickly with their easy decisions and slowly with their difficult decisions.

Knowing this, I decided to reverse this tendency, acting especially fast with my normally "difficult" decisions (weak hands) and slower with my obvious decisions (strong hands). It's worth noting that I routinely play 20 tables or more at a time online, so I am fully capable of making intelligent decisions much faster than the average player.

Another unique aspect of the Global Poker League is that the players can watch the match and find out their opponent's hole cards on a 10-minute delay. This greatly complicates matters because my opponent will see how I play specific hands and will adjust accordingly. Knowing this, I made a point to play similar hands in opposing ways, hopefully making myself difficult to read.

We battled back and forth in the initial stages of our match. Eventually I found myself with a gutshot straight draw on the flop after raising pre-flop. My opponent checked, I continuation bet, and he called. The turn was an innocuous card. We both checked. The river was another innocuous card. My opponent checked, leading me to believe he had a marginal made hand (he would likely bet with his strong value hands and bluffs). I somewhat quickly bet about 60% pot, which is the same bet size I had previously made on two occasions with decent value hands. After much deliberation, my opponent folded a marginal pair, awarding me a nice pot.

While this pot may not seem incredibly significant, *if you can use these plays to win even one additional pot each day, you'll drastically increase your win rate*. If you can accurately figure out what your opponent thinks of you or how he approaches poker, you can get well out of line and exploit his tendencies. If instead of betting fairly quickly, I'd thought for a while beforehand, I think it's likely my opponent would have called. By diligently studying my opponent before our match, I put myself in a position to steal a decent pot I would have otherwise lost.

All of this said, you have to be extremely careful when assuming you know how your opponent approaches poker. There are very few instances that arise where your opponent will actually say out loud "I think people are generally weak when they check behind quickly" or "I always make a min-reraise preflop with pocket aces." The fact that my opponent probably didn't know much about my strategies whereas I knew a decent amount about his gave me the opportunity to get out of line. Don't fall into the trap of thinking that you know what your opponents are thinking. Versus generally unknown, but competent players, acting in an unexploitable way will usually lead to the most profit in the long run.

Hand #123: Bet without putting in chips strengthens range
$550 buy-in NLHE tournament

It's the river, heads-up, and my opponent shoves for a pot-sized bet. I have a bluff catcher.

When my opponent shoves, he announces, "All-in," and sits there calmly; he doesn't put any chips into the pot.

I am getting 2:1 on the call, so my opponent has to be bluffing at least 33% of the time for this to be a good call (ignoring other possible tournament considerations). My opponent has been aggressive, and based on how the hand has gone down, I believe he's bluffing here about 40% of the time.

But when my opponent shoved, he didn't place any chips into the pot. *Not putting chips into the pot when an-*

nouncing an all-in makes strong hands more likely. It's not super-reliable, but it's enough to sway my decision if I'm on the fence.

The reason for this pattern is that bluffers often have an incentive to act confidently, and one way to act confidently is to place chips into the pot.

Another factor: *bluffers often have an incentive to make sure their bet is seen and understood.* They don't want an opponent to call because they thought the bet was less than it was.

Conversely, from the strong-hand perspective: not putting chips into the pot can be seen as a slightly impolite or goading thing to do. Moving stacks into the middle can be seen as a polite attempt at transparency, as a way of saying, "Here's my stack if you want to look at the amount." Refusing to move in chips can be seen as slightly goading, essentially saying, "You can study my chips from afar and figure it out yourself."

When working on my video series, I did an analysis of around 80 post-flop all-ins and studied if and when the players placed chips into the pot.

There was a good amount of variety, as there often is, but the things that stood out were:

- Players shoving with vulnerable hands and bluffs were significantly more likely to place chips into the pot when going all-in.

- For players shoving with clearly strong hands, it varied a lot; they were about equally likely to put in chips as not put in chips.

This general pattern jibes with my own experience at the tables.

This is a good spot to look more in-depth at how the math of a poker tell's reliability might affect a decision. Purely for argument's sake, let's say the following numbers are true for a large post-flop bet for the general recreational player population:

- Not putting chips into the pot makes it 33% less likely a bettor has a weak hand

- Putting chips into the pot makes it 10% less likely a bettor has a strong hand

This would mean, in this river situation, if I thought that my opponent had a 40% likelihood of bluffing, his behavior would reduce that likelihood by 33%, making it a 27% probability he's bluffing. This would then make a fold correct.

Note that it is far from a 100% reliable tell; it's just large enough a factor to alter a close decision.

And also note that if this player put chips into the pot, it would be even less of a factor, because he's easily capable of doing that with both strong and weak hands. If he put chips into the pot, his chances of having a strong hand would go from 60% to 54%, not as big a difference.

Obviously this is all highly theoretical, as in practice it's impossible to know in such an exact way the percentages of how someone's behavior shows up. Also, real-world behaviors and hand strength are both often non-binary, and can blur the lines between categories, making large-scale studies of this kind difficult.

I included this because it shows the mathematical logic

behind trying to make use of behavior. Whenever you use tells intelligently, and try to balance the many factors in a hand (like pot odds), these are the kinds of calculations you're doing, even if they're being done in a rough, approximate way.

Back to the hand:

I'm on the fence about calling or folding, and my opponent has announced, "All-in." Then he just sat there, putting no chips into the pot. Based on my belief that this general behavior makes strong hands significantly more likely, I fold.

My opponent turns over a bluff.

This might seem like a bad read, but that's only true if you have an overly high expectation for tells. When I acted on the behavior, I believed the pattern only decreased the chances he was bluffing by somewhere around 30%, so the results shouldn't be surprising.

Hand #124: Inconspicuous all-in strengthens range
$2-5 NLHE cash game

My opponent in this hand is short-stacked: he only has $200 to start the hand. There is one limp and he raises in middle position to $25. I call in the small blind with A♥ Q♥.

The flop is Q♣ J♣ 3♣. I check and he checks back.

The turn is the 7♦. I check and he bets $35 into $55. I call.

The river is another 3.

I check and he says, "All in," but he says it very quietly. After a few seconds pause, he starts to slide his chips into the pot. He first slides one stack of chips into the pot and then, after a few more seconds, slides the other stack. It's $140 total, into a pot of $125.

His combined river behavior is very likely to indicate a strong hand. Why is that?

Let's imagine he was bluffing. If he were bluffing, he wouldn't want to quietly announce an all-in and then only put half his stack in. If he did this, his opponent might not hear his all-in and might announce, "Call," thinking the bet was only $70 and not the full $140. If this player were bluffing, he would probably either announce "All in" clearly, or he would place his whole stack in at one time.

When a bettor doesn't seem concerned with his bet amount being clearly understood, it's a strong indicator of relaxation. This pattern holds true for any bets that could easily be missed or misinterpreted.

I fold and the player shows Q♦ Q♠ for the flopped set and rivered full house.

This pattern is related to the behavior talked about in the last hand: bluffers will usually have a motivation to a) express confidence by putting in chips, and b) want to ensure the full bet amount is clearly understood.

Some more examples of similar behavior:

- A player announces, "All in" fairly quietly and then throws a single chip into the pot.

- A player bets several stacks of chips, without stating an amount, and the stacks are positioned in such a way that his opponent might not see some of the chips. For example, the player pushes three chip stacks in, but one of the chip stacks is shorter and slightly hidden behind the other two stacks.

Quiet announcements of all-ins can be even more of a factor when the bettor's opponent is far across the table or the opponent is wearing headphones. For example, had I been wearing headphones in this hand, the bettor's behavior would seem even more relaxed, as he'd likely be even more concerned than usual that I wouldn't hear his all-in announcement.

To compare this to the behavior in the last hand (not putting in chips when going all-in) I'd say inconspicuous all-in behavior is much more likely to be reliable. I mention this just to point out that different behaviors will have different levels of reliability. I've avoided trying to rank such things in this book, as I think they can vary so much across player populations, so there's a limit to the usefulness of trying to define that kind of thing exactly.

Hand #125: Visually obscured bet makes strong hand likely

$5-10 NLHE cash game

A player bets $155 on the river into a pot of $140. His bet is arranged with $55 in red chips sitting on top of a single $100 black chip.

Similar to the last hand, this is a bet that could easily be misinterpreted by an opponent as being smaller than it actually was. The black chip could easily be overlooked, and this was especially a factor in this situation because the card room was pretty dark. This means it's likely the bettor is not concerned about a call stemming from a misunderstanding of the bet size. *Bluffers will generally be careful to ensure an opponent sees or understands the bet size.*

GABRIEL GOFFI

on neck pulse reads and scarves

The following is from a 2014 talk I had with Gabriel Goffi, a professional poker player and entrepreneur from Brazil. His website is at GabrielGoffi.com.

ELWOOD: How much do poker tells play a role in your game in general?

GOFFI: I think they're very important. There are some basic tells that have helped me a lot. For example, like the pulse in the neck. It's helped me a lot, especially against amateurs. So I could realize that they were bluffing. I've won huge pots making hero calls based on that.

Of course, it's not always 100 percent sure, but when you focus on behavior, it gives you a lot of edge on other players. A lot of players aren't looking for that. They're looking at their phones or whatever. It's powerful and has helped me a lot.

I remember one time I think my own pulse gave me away. I was playing a huge game, with stacks were like 100,000 Brazilian reais [$40,000 USD]. There was a huge fish, playing every hand, potting a lot, super aggressive.

This hand happened. I had blockers on the turn. The board was like 7-6-5. I had 99. He bets. I pot 30K on turn and he called. There was a flush draw on the flop. The river was a blank. I pot all in, like 50K reais. And he tanks.

I forgot to hide my neck and my hand was on my mouth. I was just holding still. And this guy was think-ing. He starts looking at me. I'm thinking "Of course he can't call me, he doesn't have the straight, he must have a busted flush draw or just a pair. What's he thinking?" He had been drinking, too, so it probably was a mistake on my part to try to bluff him. But long story short, he ended up calling. He called with two-pair, like 6-5.

My friend, who was on the table, said, "Gabriel, I can't believe it, man, your neck was pumping like you were going to die." And I'm pretty sure he called me because of that. He must have thought: "This guy is so nervous, he must be bluffing." After that, I made sure to always hide my neck.

ELWOOD: How do you hide your neck?

GOFFI: Different ways. Sometimes it's a scarf. Other times I just put my hand up, like Phil Hellmuth does, blocking the neck. Sometimes I put my jacket up, just to hide the neck. I diversify.

ELWOOD: Do you think that's why you see so many high-stakes poker players wearing scarves these days? Seems like it's a real fad to wear the scarves.

GOFFI: Yes, I'm pretty sure it's about that. Because, in my experience, most of the time when the pulse was pumping, it's bluffing. Unless it's an amateur who is nervous because it's a lot of money to him and he's got a strong hand. But most of the time, he's bluffing. And it's something that's really hard to control. Even if we've played five, six, ten years. It's an emotional thing and it's hard to control. And I include myself. I do a lot of yoga; I do a lot of breath exercise. And even with that, I can't control it sometimes. It's just bigger than me. My heart starts pumping and I feel uncomfortable and I have to hide.

ELWOOD: Yeah. If you're an experienced player, you're not likely to get that excited with a strong hand, because that's pretty normal and you feel comfortable. But making a big bluff can still be exciting.

GOFFI: And you just feel more protected when you hide yourself. I think that's why people use sunglasses. Because you feel comfortable. So when you hide your neck and eyes, you think "I'm in the zone." I don't use sunglasses but I think the neck is very important.

Hand #126: Excuses for strong-hand behavior

2016 European Poker Tour €5,300 buy-in NLHE tournament

This is the game-ending hand from an EPT tournament. Blinds are 300K-600K with 100K antes.

Sebastian Malec limps with A♥ 3♥ on the button. Uri Reichenstein checks the big blind with T♥ 9♣.

The flop is Q♥ J♠ 6♥. Reichenstein bets 800K and Malec raises to 3M. Reichenstein calls.

Throughout this hand and in some previous hands, Malec has been standing up periodically and rocking back and forth. He had been saying that he had to go to the bathroom.

The turn is the 8♥, giving Reichenstein a straight and Malec the flush. Reichenstein checks and Malec bets 5M. As Reichenstein calls, Malec talks quite a bit. One thing he says is, "Just fold and I can go to the bathroom." Another thing he says is, "You don't have any strong hands when you just lead like… I'm pretty sure you're going to just fold, so…"

Reichenstein calls.

The river is the 8♦, so the board is Q♥ J♠ 6♥ 8♥ 8♦.

Reichenstein checks and Malec says "All-in" after a couple seconds. He covers Reichenstein's remaining 17.5M.

As Reichenstein thinks, Malec says, "I think I cover, right? So you call and it's all over, baby. Like Scotty Nguyen, eh?"

Malec is implying that he has a strong hand. He's referencing a well-known poker hand where Scotty Nguyen said, "You call and it's all over, baby," and Nguyen did have a strong hand.

At this point, Malec is standing up and gesturing in a physically loose way.

Reichenstein: "It's so sick you're telling the truth and my hand is insanely strong."

Malec: "I mean, you don't have any strong hands. How could you have a strong hand, like, you lead, like, never a strong hand, never a strong hand. So, just fold and I can go to the bathroom."

Reichenstein: "It's like, I have a hand that's impossible to fold. But everything you say just makes it slightly possible."

Malec: "I mean, like, I just want to go pee-pee. I really want to pee, so... I'm just convinced, like, like... I don't know. I guess you could have like nine-ten or something."

Reichenstein: "What about nine-ten? Is nine-ten good?"

Malec: "It's a straight. But like, I have Queens in my range. Jacks. Sixes. You don't have those hands in your range."

Reichenstein: "I don't think you have any of those hands. I think you might have a flush, though."

Malec: "Yeah, I think I have, like, maybe I have sixes,

but I raise sixes, right, so? Yeah... It's your choice, man."

Reichenstein: "It's so sick. Nobody ever talks like you without having the hand. It's so sick."

At this point, Malec walks away from the table and interacts with people on the rail, talking to them. He talks about how he's going to be the winner, and says, "EPT champion over here."

Reichenstein ends up making the call and Malec shows the nut flush.

While Reichenstein seemed to interpret many of Malec's behaviors as indicating a strong hand, it's possible Malec had acted so loose and unusual throughout the game that he decided to overlook Malec's behavior. (There was also a hand where Malec bet trips on the river and remained calm and quiet for quite a while; this may have thrown off Reichenstein's read and made him think Malec was more likely to be quiet with strong hands.) Having said that, in my quick review of the hour before this hand, I saw nothing resembling the behavioral looseness of Malec in this hand.

Let's look at some of the more pertinent behaviors:

- **Talkativeness after making a big bet.** It's the rare player who can be so loquacious after betting. Loose, relaxed talking from someone who's made a big bet (i.e., the "speech") will usually represent relaxation. This is especially true the more amateur the player is, as most amateur players aren't comfortable talking so much when bluffing.

- **Talking about the play of the hand.** As I wrote in *Verbal Poker Tells*, even if a player is willing to talk when bluffing, that talking will usually consist of rather neutral, non-confrontational speech. When a player is willing to talk about the strategy of the hand, and the ranges of hands possible, it is a reliable tell that that player is relaxed.

- **Goading.** Goading language like "Just fold and I can go to the bathroom" is unlikely to be said by a bluffer. Even a bluffer who wants to talk will usually not choose such confrontational language that might accidentally result in a "spite-call."

- **Misdirections/excuses explaining strong-hand behavior.** The most interesting part of their verbal interaction is when Reichenstein says, "I have a hand that's impossible to fold. But everything you say just makes it slightly possible." *At this accusation that he (Malec) is acting in a way that screams strength, Malec essentially makes excuses for his behavior.* If Malec were bluffing, he would have no incentive to lead Reichenstein away from the idea that he had a strong hand. This, to me, is the strongest evidence by far that Malec has a strong hand and wants a call.

- **Standing up and walking around.** In my database, I have notes on several years' worth of WSOP footage, and I did an analysis of all the post-flop, post-bet situations where the bettors stood up. (The compilation video is on my Youtube channel: YouTube.com/readingpokertells.) *In almost every case of post-bet standing, the bettor was strong.* In this hand, though, the standing wouldn't be considered a factor, as Malec often stood in many hands and in several spots throughout this hand. On the other hand, Malec also walked away and interacted with the rail, which was unusual and relaxed-seeming even taking into account his previous behavior.

All of these behaviors combined would make me very confident Malec was relaxed and had at least a flush. If I were Reichenstein, I would have to have seen Malec exhibit a lot of stereotypical strong-hand behavior when bluffing to ever get me to want to call this bet. (And in Reichenstein's defense, perhaps he'd seen Malec do that earlier; I did not watch all the footage.)

If you liked this analysis and haven't yet read my book *Verbal Poker Tells*, I recommend it. It contains a lot of during-hand statement analysis like this.

Hand #127: Conciliatory smile and language help sway decision

$2-5 NLHE cash game

I raise to $15 with K♣ Q♣ and get five callers.

The flop is Q♠ 9♣ 7♠. I bet $50 into $90 and get two callers.

The turn is the 9♦. I check, the second player checks, and the third player, a stranger to me, bets $75 into $240. I call.

The river is the 5♠. I check and my opponent bets $260 into $390.

I look at him and he stares steadily back at me in a neutral way.

I ask him, "You want a call?"

He says quickly, "It's up to you," and smiles slightly in a

friendly way. I call and he mucks.

Players with strong hands are more likely to act in subdued, unhappy, or even unfriendly ways, in order to get calls. Bluffing players are more likely to act in conciliatory, friendly, and neutral ways.

In this case, I thought his friendly, neutral language and his small, friendly smile made it more likely he was bluffing. This isn't a very reliable read, but *if I'm on the fence in what I think is a borderline spot, these kinds of small clues can sway me one way or the other.*

In this case, his post-bet eye contact didn't mean much to me. For one thing, he was a stranger to me, and eye contact tells can vary a lot from person to person. I'd want to get a sense of a player's post-bet eye contact before acting on it.

Also, his staring was very neutral and consistent; if he'd had a lot of back-and-forth eye contact, looking to me and away from me and back again, I'd be more likely to interpret that as being relaxed. But a consistent, stoic look can easily be from either a bluffer or a value-bettor.

LIMON
on actors vs. non-actors

The following is from a 2014 talk I had with "Limon," who's been playing mid- to high-stakes L.A. poker games for a living since 2004.

He's a regular host for the online poker show *Live At The Bike* (LiveAtTheBike.com), which features cash game footage from the Bicycle Casino in L.A., along with commentary. He's also available for poker coaching in the L.A. area.

ELWOOD: How important are tells in the big scheme of things?

LIMON: Well, you don't need to know anything about tells to win money at poker. I play with some guys who are very, very good players. Some of them don't even believe that tells exist. I mean, they know they exist, but they don't think that they're worth figuring out.

This is true for a lot of the younger, more anti-social guys coming into the game. Sometimes it's not just that they don't want to learn tells; but that they can't do it. For the same reason they can't tell that a girl likes them. There's just a whole bunch of stuff they don't know.

So you can win a lot of money and not focus on this stuff. But if you're not focusing on this stuff you definitely are leaving money on the table. In my PLO game, I'm probably the biggest winner. And I'm probably not the most experienced PLO player in the world, but I think the gap where I make more money is definitely the things I notice about my opponents. I'd say it's a solid extra, maybe 15 percent. So I think it's worth it.

ELWOOD: What role would you say tells play in your poker game?

LIMON: They play a lot in mine, for sure. The nature of PLO, the nuts are changing on every street; things change a lot more than in Hold'em. People's reactions are a lot more genuine. You see a lot more gut reactions.

They don't have time to develop a game plan. If you're familiar with the game and you're thinking one step ahead already, you get a ton of information from people who aren't thinking one step ahead.

ELWOOD: What's an example of a tell in PLO you've used recently?

LIMON: Well, one is, because you can only bet the size of the pot, people say "pot" a lot. And one of the first things you figure out, is when someone always says "pot" and then don't say "pot," you want to correlate that. Or if you never hear them say "pot" and then you hear them say "pot." That's like your first PLO tell; baby's first tell.

After that it gets more complicated, but in general, it's the same kind of stuff you wrote about in your book [*Reading Poker Tells*]. There are polarized behaviors. Like if you check to a guy and he grabs a bunch of chips and he doesn't count them and just puts them in the pot; that is 100% a tell of some sort. And it's usually a tell of one of two things; he's either got the nuts or he's bluffing.

Because you know that that's a tell of some sort, you have to suss out whether the guy's acting or not. If the guy puts in a bunch of chips nonchalantly and he's acting, he will continue to try to act nonchalant. If the guy puts in a stack of chips because he has the nuts, he will not continue to act; it wasn't an act in the first place. It was more like a sigh of relief. If he puts in the chips and has no act after it, he just sort of sits still or has just random eye movements or whatever, he's got the nuts. He didn't have an act planned out and took a random amount of chips because he didn't give a shit.

A guy who's bluffing has an act and he's thought it out beforehand and he's gonna try and do it. He has a script. A guy with the nuts doesn't have a script; he'll bounce around all over the place. But a guy bluffing has a script. And he's afraid to go off-script.

The best is when a guy does something weird and then turns instantly as his food's being dropped off and tells the server that they forgot his pickle; something like that. That guy is never fucking bluffing. Because he's in the moment. He's completely in the moment. He's not thinking about acting. He notices out of the corner of his eye that they brought his ham sandwich with no pickle and goes, "Server, server, you forgot the pickle!" That kind of stuff happens all the time.

I will say that younger professional players are really good at disguising their tells in general. Most of them have watched Durrrr *[pro player Tom Dwan's screen name]* play and have copied the way he played. Which is to do the same thing every single time. It does make it tough because they're not giving out much.

Hand #128: A false tell gone wrong

$2-5 NLHE cash game

This hand took place when I played on the poker show *Live At The Bike*.

Cyrus Nemani is a player who I've only played a few hands with in the last few minutes, but who I think is a good player. He also knows that I've written books on poker tells.

He raises on the button to $15. I have A♠ K♥ in the big

blind and make it $50. He calls.

The flop is 5♣ 2♣ 2♠. I bet $60 into $105. He calls.

The turn is 6♦. I check. He bets $120 into $225. I call.

The river is the Q♣, putting three clubs out. I immediately check and Cyrus bets $300 into $465. I considered calling, as I know I'm often ahead, but I fold.

He later tells me that my immediate check encouraged him to bluff. He had A♥ 9♦.

This makes sense. Immediate checks will usually mean that a person doesn't have a reason to think. In this case, one would think if I'd rivered a flush, I'd have an incentive to think for a moment about what to do.

What was actually happening was a little more complex. Sometimes, if I think an opponent is decent and I think they perceive me as decent, I will check quickly to them when I want to discourage them from bluffing. My idea is that, because a quick check seems unusual and like something a decent player wouldn't want to do with a weak hand, I might make my opponent worried that I'm trying to induce a bluff with the intention of calling.

In this case, I also was encouraged to do this because I knew that Cyrus knew I wrote about poker tells, so I was hoping he'd think something like, "Oh, he's trying to induce me and plans on snap-calling, I shouldn't bluff here."

But this is clearly all too fancy for my own good. Most thinking players will interpret a quick check on the river as likely to indicate a weak hand, and most thinking players would be encouraged to bluff, as Cyrus was here. This was revealed as kind of a weird blind spot for me: I typically never try to do these kinds of weird reverse-psychology ploys unless I have a few reasons to do them.

This shows the difficulties of trying to use false tells. *Most of the time, we have no idea how our opponents will interpret our behavior or act on it.* Sometimes we think someone will probably interpret something one way and they'll interpret it the opposite way.

Cyrus, on reading this hand later, said: it's not a good idea to perform a false tell that essentially "caps your range" (i.e., limits the strength of your hand). And that's also a good point.

Hand #129: Deprecating comment from bettor strengthens range

$2-5 NLHE cash game

It's a limped multiway pot. I have A♠ T♠.

The flop is J♥ 7♣ 5♠ and it's checked around.

The turn is the A♥. An early position player bets $15 into $30. I call.

An aggressive player raises to $50. The first bettor folds. I call.

The river is the 3♣. I check. He bets $100 into $145.

I'm on the fence here, as this could easily go either way. I ask him, "What do you have?"

He says, "I misplayed my hand, I'll tell you that."

This is similar to making a weak-hand statement: *Bluffers generally don't want to imply something that might make an opponent suspicious.* In this case, if he were bluffing, he wouldn't want to express confusion about the hand, and he wouldn't want to make me focus on how he's played the hand.

I fold. He shows 7♥ 5♠, for two pair. He explains that

he got distracted on the flop or he would have bet.

A lot of the most useful verbal behavior happens on the river. When all the decisions are over, sometimes players with strong hands feel relaxed enough to talk, and sometimes these statements will give away their lack of concern about the situation.

Kassouf and his speech play in 2016 WSOP ME

In the 2016 WSOP Main Event, William Kassouf received a lot of coverage for his frequent during-hand chatter. Some people found his "speech play" (as they like to call it in Europe) annoying and rude; some people thought it was fun and made the coverage more watchable. This was reminiscent of Jamie Gold's talkative performance in 2006, with the same polarized opinions.

I found a good amount of reliable patterns in Kassouf's talk. And these are also patterns that are common amongst amateur players, so they're worth understanding.

First, let's look at Kassouf's general modus operandi. Kassouf liked to ramble verbally in many spots and most of this patter was made up of strong-hand statements. Here are some examples, which Kassouf repeated in various iterations many times:

- "I think I'm ahead."

- "Get my money in good, that's all I can do."

- "I'm not bluffing."

- "I've got a legitimate hand this time."

Strong-hand statements are hard to interpret because players with both strong hands and weak hands are capable of making strong-hand statements. Bluffers understandably want to imply strength about their hand. But players betting strong hands are sometimes just very relaxed and don't mind implying strength about their hand (and sometimes they're purposefully trying to "level" an opponent to induce a suspicious call).

It makes sense that Kassouf's patter, and most talkative player's patter in general, consists mostly of strong-hand statements. Most hands played by the average, decently-aggressive player are not that strong. There are a lot of weak and medium-strength hands. So, in most spots, these players are happy taking the pot down pre-flop or on the flop. And it's even more true in the WSOP Main Event, where tournament life has additional meta-value due to media attention and exposure. Strong-hand statements discourage action more than weak-hand statements do, so it makes sense they would be instinctually chosen for general verbal "filler" purposes.

Another reason strong-hand statements are chosen for such general during-hand talking is that they do have actual defensive value. This is because people don't like to be fooled. People don't like to be told by an opponent "I've got a strong hand," ignore that warning, and then be shown a strong hand.

For example, when a player like Kassouf three-bets you and tells you, "I've got a big hand now, big hand," even if you know such chatter from him is generally meaningless and balanced, you'd hate to shove and have him actually show down a big hand. The verbal aspect adds a little extra drama to the situation. For many players, the situation will sting more when it feels like they've been tricked.

These things affect recreational players more than skilled players, of course, but taken as a whole, these kinds of statements do slow players down more than you'd think.

Knowing that Kassouf's general chatter consists of many strong-hand statements, and that these can be present with both weak hands and strong hands, my analysis consisted of studying his weak-hand statements. As you probably know by now, weak-hand statements accompanying bets are highly correlated with strong hands. This pattern held up quite well for Kassouf: *when he bet and his speech contained weak-hand statements, he would usually have a strong hand.* And the more weak-hand statements he made, the more likely it became that he really did have a strong hand.

There were quite a few hands featuring Kassouf in that event, but we'll look at only two here: a value-bet and a bluff.

The straight flush

In this hand, Kassouf turned a straight flush versus a player named Stacy Matuson.

Kassouf had 9♥ 6♥ on a turn board of A♦ 8♥ 7♥ 5♥. Matuson had A♠ Q♠.

Kassouf checked the turn and Matuson bet 225K into a pot of 640K. Kassouf shoved for Matuson's remaining 925K. He talked a lot before he raised and after. Here are a few of the weak-hand statements he made, along with comments:

- **"You going to keep bluffing me?"** Kassouf says this before he shoves. By implying that he thinks his opponent might be bluffing, Kassouf weakens his perceived range. If you believe your opponent is bluffing, you don't need a strong hand to shove with.

- **"I can't call. There's only one million in the pot you only have six or seven [hundred thousand] behind."** Kassouf says this as an apparent explanation for why he'd shove instead of calling. (Matuson informs him she actually has 900,000 behind.) When players make excuses for their actions, it will usually be a misdirection, directing attention away from the true reasons for the decision.

- **"I know what she has, anyway: she's got top pair with a heart draw."** Kassouf says this after shoving and talking to Matuson for a while. In this context, a single pair seems pretty weak on a three-flush board. Stating that an opponent has a weak hand is a goading behavior. It also, after a bet, implies comfort with the situation.

- **"You playing to ladder up or you playing to win? I'm playing to win so I play for it all."** This is both goading and a weak-hand statement. Kassouf is reminding Matuson that in a tournament you have to be willing to take chances to win. And he's implying that he's willing to take chances, to put in his money in questionable spots, in order to try to win.

- **"You're probably ahead."** Kassouf says this a couple times. It's rare for a bluffer to make such direct weak-hand statements like this.

- **"You want to gamble, young lady? Yes or no?"** He

asks this before shoving. While a bit ambiguous, it seems to imply that he thinks the winner could easily be either one of them. It implies that Matuson has a shot at winning, and this weakens Kassouf's range. This was one of two hands I saw where Kassouf used a phrase like "Let's gamble" when betting or raising; the other one was when he three-bet pre-flop with pocket aces. In this hand he says the word gamble more than fourteen times.

"Nine-high like a boss" bluff

In this hand, Kassouf bluffs the river versus the same player, Stacy Matuson. He has 9♥ 6♣ and the river board is 5♦ 3♥ 2♣ 8♥ T♠. Matuson has Q♠ Q♦.

Kassouf talks a good amount here. His speech contains strong-hand statements and neutral statements. There are no clear weak-hand statements, like there were in the previous hand.

His speech includes these statements:

- **"There's over 600K in there, so I want you to call."** A very direct strong-hand statement.

- **"If you fold, I'll show, but I want you to call 100 percent."** Another very direct strong-hand statement.

- **"Don't want to bust out with the whole camera crew watching. That will be embarrassing."** In the previous hand, Kassouf said you "have to gamble to win" a tournament, whereas here he is drawing attention to the negative aspect of taking a chance and losing.

- **"You don't put me on this hand, I'll tell you."** A bit ambiguous, but indirectly implies strength.

- **"I'm not trying to bust you."** He says something similar several times. This is a conciliatory statement. Often bluffers, if they're motivated to talk, will do so but in friendly, conciliatory ways. Conciliatory behavior is basically the opposite of goading behavior; it is aimed at reducing conflict and agitation.

These two hands are representative of Kassouf's patterns, and of talkative player patterns in general:

- If his speech when betting contained weak-hand statements or goading statements, *it was likely he had a strong hand*. The more weak-hand statements there were, the more likely a strong hand became.

- If his speech had no weak-hand statements or goading statements—or almost none—*it was likely he was bluffing*.

What made Kassouf's verbal tells so actionable was that his speeches contained multiple points of reference. If Kassouf had only said one or two hand-strength statements during these hands, it would be much harder to get a confident read. The main reason being that strong-hand statements can be said with both strong hands and weak hands, so one or two strong-hand statements wouldn't contain much information.

But multiple clues can add up to paint a reliable picture. The more Kassouf spoke without making a weak-hand statement, the more likely it became that he was bluffing. The more weak-hand statements he made, the more likely it became that he had a strong hand.

This shows the downside of talking a lot during hands. It's more difficult than most people realize to stay balanced and not have some sort of pattern show up when you are talking a lot, or engaging frequently in any unusual behavior.

If you'd like to learn more about Kassouf's tells in that WSOP, do an online search for 'Kassouf poker tells' and you should find a PokerNews article I wrote that goes into more detail on these hands and two others. It also includes a video compilation.

Hand #130: Relief after all-in isn't snap-called

2016 European Poker Tour NLHE €10,300 buy-in tournament

The blinds are 30K/60K, with a 5K ante.

Fedor Holz limps in the cut-off with Q♥ T♥. The blinds come along. Chance Kornuth is in the big blind.

The flop is 4♣ 4♦ 2♣. The small blind checks. Kornuth bets 120K and Holz calls.

The turn is the 2♦. Kornuth bets 325K. Holz calls.

The river is the 7♦. Kornuth shoves, and he covers Holz's 1.2M stack.

After a moment, Kornuth says, "I'm just happy you didn't snap call."

Holz ends up calling with Q high and Kornuth shows Q-2 for twos full of fours.

Sometimes players will make an all-in bet or raise with a strong hand that could easily be behind. *When these players don't get an immediate call from an opponent, they are capable of letting out genuine expressions of relief because the hands they were most afraid of are no longer possible.*

The fact that a bettor is willing to talk at all, and especially that he's willing to express some concern about his own hand, makes it likely that the player is relaxed. If a player who bets all-in was bluffing, he'd be unlikely to make a statement that communicates "I was sweating that one" because such a statement seems to subtract the strongest hands from his own range. And, as discussed at length in *Verbal Poker Tells*, bluffers generally don't like to make weak-hand statements.

In regards to this hand: in a vacuum, not knowing anything about their history or the skill of the players, I'd be very confident that this was a strong hand. A bluffer, even if he's a good player, is hardly ever going to want to make a weak-hand statement like this. Even assuming both players are strong players and both know that this statement is usually a sign of relaxation (which makes it possible there'll be some leveling), most players would not want to accidentally make an opponent suspicious. Most good players are going to either be silent or be more neutral in their verbal statements.

When I posted this hand on my blog, someone asked me if I thought good players would be more balanced and tricky with this kind of behavior. This is a common question, as people often assume that experienced players will often switch things up. *Good players are generally behaviorally balanced, but mostly in that they attempt to be consistently stoic;* it doesn't mean that good players will often try to pull off complex, verbally tricky things, especially when bluffing.

For one thing, if Kornuth was going to make such a statement when bluffing, he'd have to be confident that Holz would usually interpret that statement as indicating a strong hand. And predicting what an opponent will think of our behavior is difficult. This is especially true when both players are experienced.

This helps explain why weak-hand verbal statements like this one, even from good players, will usually happen when the player has a strong hand and is relaxed enough to try something tricky.

I will say that, in both players' defense, there could have been some verbal interactions between them that led to both of them taking these approaches. For example, maybe Kornuth had made similar weak-hand statements when bluffing in earlier hands.

But in a vacuum, and unless there was some strong evidence to the contrary, I'd be confident Kornuth was strong here.

Hand #131: A defensive obstacle-to-a-call tell from Jamie Gold

2006 WSOP NLHE $10K Main Event, final table

On a river board of 8♥ 8♦ 3♦ 2♣ Q♠, Allen Cunningham checks with A♥ 9♦ and Jamie Gold quickly bluffs with his T♦ 7♦.

After a few seconds, Cunningham says, "You just might have a Queen. Can't help it."

Gold says, "You have a Queen?"

Cunningham shrugs and says, "Maybe."

Gold says, "I'll show you. I've been showing a lot of

bluffs; I don't mind showing."

Cunningham: "I was thinking of calling it anyway."

Gold says, "All right," and grabs his cards as if ready to turn them over, but he doesn't turn them over.

Cunningham: "Oh wait—I didn't call yet."

After a few more seconds, Cunningham does call.

In talking about the hand years later, Cunningham said: "He seemed to be telling the truth a lot. I was going to call anyway, but just for fun I thought I'd talk to him a bit, do a little dance…"

Referencing Gold's reaching-for-cards behavior, Cunningham said, "They're not gonna show you their hand if they have it; so that's just a classic tell that means they're bluffing."

Hand #132: Honest statement weakens range

$1-2 NLHE cash game

I have T♣ T♦ and turn a full house on a board of K♣ T♥ 5♦ 5♥.

My opponent checks to me and I bet $25 into $50. He calls.

The river is the K♥, putting out a second King and three hearts. My opponent bets all-in for his last $60 into a $100 pot.

My opponent is a tight player who I think would be very unlikely to be bluffing here, making his range mostly polarized between either having a King or not. At the same time, he strikes me as bad enough that he might weirdly do this with some strong hands that I beat.

I ask him, "Do you have a King?"

He says, "No."

I ask, "You promise?"

He says, "Yes, I promise."

I call and he shows Q♥ J♥ for the flush. This makes sense; this hand is probably the one hand that he plays in such a way that I beat.

When it comes to very clear and direct hand-strength statements, most players will be quite truthful. This was an interesting spot where my opponent interpreted my apparent uncertainty as indicating he must be ahead with his flush, which made him willing to be truthful about his hand and remove a king from his range. He didn't realize that a King was the only hand I was afraid of.

SHANIAC

on poker tells and the state of the game

Shane Schleger, also known by his online handle Shaniac, has been playing poker professionally since before 2005. This is taken from a talk I had with him in 2015.

ELWOOD: How important is studying opponent behavior to your game?

SCHLEGER: It's something you want to try to tune into. It's often subtle. And it's just one aspect of live poker. It's rare you find extreme value, but it can be valuable. If you're paying attention to subtle things, like whether someone's talking or not talking, such things can definitely point you in the right direction. But I use it in combination with whatever else is going on in the game, strategy-wise and tempo-wise. You ideally want to incorporate everything: strategy, body language, actual language. There are so many factors. It's more of a holistic way of looking at a poker hand.

That's a big part of why it's good to cultivate the social aspect of the game. For example, you can sometimes get a sense of how a person feels about their place in the game. An obvious example of where this comes in handy is in bubble situations in tournaments. I do believe in connecting the human element to the logic of what is going on in the hand.

ELWOOD: Do you think poker, as it's become more solved and studied now, and as they get closer to GTO solutions, is it becoming more boring? And do you think we'll see the death of poker as it becomes more solved?

SCHLEGER: I don't want to be dramatic. It's unfortunate, I guess, that it's become a game of studiousness. There was a nice aspect to poker, that anyone could play, and you didn't have to feel that you were engaged in an intellectual competition. There was at least the illusion that there was a level playing field. Now there's such an emphasis on learning and studying and making the right play. It's become a very coaching- and knowledge-intensive sort of game, so I don't know if there's a way to step back from that.

ELWOOD: Something I was thinking about: people worry that certain things give poker a dark or dangerous image. But in my experience that's actually what many recreational players enjoy about poker. It's got this romantic, dark history and some players are excited by poker because it feels like they're doing something edgy and semi-dangerous. Regular players love to tell stories about all the degenerate, weird characters they've met and played with. For a lot of poker players, that's a draw for them, too.

SCHLEGER: I tend to agree. It gets really old, this talk of the ethics of playing against problem gamblers or weaker players. That is the thing about poker: you have to decide your own level of risk tolerance and degeneracy. You have to regulate your poker habit. I don't think there should be any nannying that takes place in poker. If someone wants to come to the table and that's how they want to pass their time, who says they have to be doing yoga or something traditionally "happy." I agree. That is part of the allure: figuring out your risk tolerance and adjusting.

ELWOOD: You could definitely make an analogy between drugs and poker.

SCHLEGER: For sure. Gambling is a drug, and poker is a drug. It's reinforcing highs and lows basically in every hand. In that, it provides a certain amount of escapism. It's natural to want to experience that edge or that risk. It's certainly related to drugs; I just don't make the negative association. Poker is a drug. There's definitely a compulsive element to it. And you have to embrace that and regulate it, just like many other things in life. Like food, exercise, sex, drugs.

But the game has changed into, kind of, the poker nerds versus the sad sacks who don't understand game theory. It should be more like: if you have an edge, you enjoy it quietly instead of bragging about how much you know.

It's an ethic that's sort of been lost. People don't understand why it's important to preserve a more pleasant
illusion of the game. The recreational player will return
as long as he thinks the game is fair and as long as he isn't
made to feel like a fool. No one wants to be made to feel
like a fool.

ELWOOD: And for me it's just a polite thing. It's not like
I'm even worried about the state of the game, because I
think the game will mainly be what it is. But it just feels
wrong to shove it in the faces of people who are just there
to have a good time.

SCHLEGER: There are so many players who base their
confidence and sense of belonging on their poker skills.
So it's hard to separate these concepts that we're talking
about. So it's like: "Fuck the fish, they're not going to get
better anyway." So some things get passed over in this
younger, more intellectually aggressive game.

Erik Seidel is a good example of someone who had a
public image, but maintained the mystery of poker,
never talked negatively about his opponents, never
talked positively about his skill or his accomplishments,
was always sort of like: "Get it quietly, keep people guess-
ing." I guess that's why he's sort of my role model. Get it
quietly.

Conclusion

I hope this book has helped you think more about the many factors to consider when trying to find and exploit behavioral patterns. It's not just a matter of acting on simple "this means that"-type reads. Instead, it's a situation-dependent process where you might take into account many things, such as:

- Fundamental strategy
- An opponent's playing style
- An opponent's past behavior
- The round of play
- The board texture

You might find it useful to go back to the *General Concepts* section at the start of the book and review those ideas. Those general concepts might make more sense now that you've read about the specific tells.

I hope you've enjoyed this book and, if you've purchased them, my other books and videos. If you feel you've gotten value from this book, please consider leaving me a book review on an online seller site like *Amazon* or *Barnes & Noble*. I self-publish my books and do all the marketing myself, so online reviews and recommendations are the main way people hear about my books. And if you didn't know, you can leave book reviews on sites like Amazon even if you didn't buy the book there.

If you've enjoyed this book, you'd also like my video series, available at www.ReadingPokerTells.video. The series analyzes footage from cash games and tournaments and shows real-world examples of the tells in my books. Many people have told me that seeing these video examples is super-helpful in improving at tell-reading. The Lifetime Membership price will continue to rise as I add more content over time, so the sooner you purchase it, the better deal you'll be getting.

Finally, if you've gotten value from my products far and above what they cost, and you want to send me a tip, I'm not too proud to accept it. I've had a lot of players tell me my content has improved their game a lot, and some people also tell me I price my content too low. If you want to send me a thank-you gift on PayPal, you can use the email address info@readingpokertells.com.

Contact and feedback

If there's anything you'd like to talk to me about, whether it's sharing a hand history, an error in the book, questions about my stuff, or just wanting to say hello, I'd love to hear from you:

Email: info@ReadingPokerTells.com
Twitter: Twitter.com/apokerplayer
Facebook: Facebook.com/ReadingPokerTells
Instagram: Instagram.com/ReadingPokerTells

Poker Tells Quiz

In my previous poker tells books, I've avoided including quizzes. The main reason is because I don't like to imply that there is a single correct way of thinking about poker tells. I also think taking tests on complex, contextual content like this can emphasize rote memorization and result in a simplistic understanding, whereas the goal should be to encourage you to make your own observations and reach your own conclusions.

But I've had a lot of readers tell me quizzes would be appreciated, and I finally agreed that a well thought-out quiz would be helpful. I've tried my best to make the quiz reinforce the concepts I'm most confident are valuable. But please keep in mind these are still just my own opinions, and I don't claim to be infallible.

A few points about this quiz:

- All questions are assumed to be about general player behavior in a vacuum (i.e., no prior reads).

- All questions are assumed to be about the most common amateur player patterns.

- All questions and answers are based on information in this book.

Note: This quiz is also online, and includes end-of-test feedback on your answers. You can take the online test here: ReadingPokerTells.com/quiz.

1. A player limps early. *He throws his chips in with a lot of forward movement, double-checks his cards, and starts talking to his neighbor.*

   This behavior makes a strong hand...
   - a. more likely than usual
   - b. less likely than usual

2. Pre-flop, a player on the button *looks at his cards and stares at them for a few seconds.* When action gets to him, he raises.

   This behavior makes a strong hand...
   - a. more likely than usual
   - b. less likely than usual

3. Pre-flop, a player raises and another player behind him calls, *saying, "Call."*

   This verbal call makes a strong hand...
   - a. more likely than usual
   - b. less likely than usual

4. Pre-flop, a player *starts to reach for chips before the player in front of him has folded.* He then raises.

   This behavior makes a strong hand...
   - a. more likely than usual
   - b. less likely than usual

5. Pre-flop, it is your turn to act. A player behind you looks at his cards. *After looking at his cards, he places a chip on his cards and turns to stare at you as it's your turn to act.*

   This player's behavior makes a strong hand...
      a. more likely than usual
      b. less likely than usual

6. Pre-flop, a player *raises immediately* when action gets to him.

   This immediate raise makes a strong hand...
      a. more likely than usual
      b. less likely than usual

7. Of the reliable poker tells you'll find from non-aggressors and waiting-to-act players, most will be tells indicating _____.

      a. weak hands
      b. strong hands

8. Of the reliable poker tells you'll find from players making large bets, most will indicate _____.

      a. weak hands
      b. strong hands

9. In a tournament, a player with only 10 BBs *waits an abnormally long time before shoving pre-flop.*

   This pause before shoving with a short stack makes a strong hand...

   a. more likely than usual

   b. less likely than usual

10. A player raises pre-flop. You and another player call. As the flop is being dealt, *the pre-flop raiser says, "No respect, huh?" and laughs.*

    This verbal behavior makes a strong hand...

    a. more likely than usual

    b. less likely than usual

11. Pre-flop, a player raises. You three-bet and your opponent *immediately calls.*

    This player isn't very good but he seems to be at least thoughtful about the game. What types of hands are made most likely by this quick call?

    a. Around AQ-AT

    b. Decent suited connectors

    c. Pairs around 99-55

    d. TT-QQ, sometimes AK

12. In a multi-way pot, on a flop of 9-9-6, *a player checks by slamming his hand down forcefully on the table.*

   This behavior makes this player having a 9...
   a. more likely than usual
   b. less likely than usual

13. It's heads-up on the flop. Your opponent *double-checks his cards* and then checks.

   This behavior makes a strong hand...
   a. more likely than usual
   b. less likely than usual

14. On the river, your opponent *double-checks his cards* and then bets.

   This behavior makes a strong hand...
   a. more likely than usual
   b. less likely than usual

15. It's heads-up on the flop. Your opponent checks to you, *saying, "Go ahead, you win."*

   This behavior makes a strong hand...
   a. more likely than usual
   b. less likely than usual

16. It's three-way to the flop. The flop is Q♥ J♥ 9♥. *A player exclaims, "Wow!"*

This behavior makes a strong hand…

  a. more likely than usual

  b. less likely than usual

17. It's heads-up on a flop of J♥ T♥ 3♠. Your opponent is an aggressive player. You continuation-bet and your opponent *calls immediately.*

Which of the following hands does this immediate call make less likely?

  a. Flush draws

  b. Open-ended straight draws

  c. Sets

  d. All of above

18. It's heads-up on a flop of J♥ T♥ 3♠. Your opponent is a passive player. You continuation-bet and *your opponent calls immediately.*

Compared to a snap-call from an aggressive player, how does this player's passivity affect his range of possible hands?

  a. His range has more flush draws and straight draws than the aggressive player's range.

  b. His range has fewer flush draws and straight draws than the aggressive player's range.

19. You are the pre-flop raiser. It's heads-up.
Your opponent, who normally acts quickly, takes a long time to check to you.

Which of the following is the more accurate analysis?
  a. It indicates some interest and makes it more likely than usual he will put more money into the pot.

  b. It indicates an attempt at intimidation and makes it less likely than usual he will call a flop bet.

20. It's heads-up on the flop. The pre-flop raiser continuation-bets and you call. On the turn, you check and the pre-flop raiser checks back. *He breaks out of his previously stoic pose and starts to move around in his seat, looking around the room.*

This behavior makes a strong hand...
  a. more likely than usual

  b. less likely than usual

21. It's heads-up. The flop is A♠ K♦ 5♣. The pre-flop raiser, an amateur player, *checks back immediately.*

This behavior makes a strong hand...
  a. more likely than usual

  b. less likely than usual

22. On a 3-way flop, you bet, and the second player raises. The third player, who is fairly tight, *quickly and casually calls, without much apparent thought.*

   This behavior makes a strong hand…

   a. more likely than usual

   b. less likely than usual

23. It's heads-up. The flop has just come out. The pre-flop raiser *studies your stack in an ostentatious way.* Then he checks to you.

   This behavior makes a strong hand…

   a. more likely than usual

   b. less likely than usual

24. It's a limped 4-way pot. On a flop of 5♦ 4♠ 4♦, the second-to-act player *immediately bets.*

   This behavior makes the bettor having a very strong hand…

   a. more likely than usual

   b. less likely than usual

25. When someone calls for a card (for example, yelling "Eight!" when the turn is coming out), what is the most accurate analysis of this behavior?

   a. It will usually be said completely truthfully.

   b. It will likely be a total lie and not at all related to

what the player wants.

c. It will likely not be extremely honest but will contain some indirect truth.

d. These statements are usually completely meaningless.

26. On the turn, in a 3-way pot, you check. The second-to-act opponent, who is sitting beside you, acts confused, *saying, "Oh, you checked?"* Then he bets.

This behavior makes a strong hand...

a. more likely than usual

b. less likely than usual

27. It's heads-up. On the turn, you check. Your opponent takes a long time to act. While he thinks, *he flips a chip end over end in his hand.* This is unusual behavior for him; usually he is very stoic. Eventually he bets.

This behavior makes a strong hand...

a. more likely than usual

b. less likely than usual

28. It's heads-up. On the river, your opponent bets. As you think, *you see that his leg is shaking below the table.*

This behavior makes a strong hand...

a. more likely than usual

b. less likely than usual

29. On a turn of A♦ Q♠ 5♣ 9♠, your opponent goes all-in. You ask him, "You have Ace-King?" *He says, "No."*

   This verbal statement makes a strong hand...

   a. more likely than usual

   b. less likely than usual

30. It's heads-up. The turn board is Q♦ 9♠ 3♦ A♠. You bet and your opponent calls. Before the river is dealt, *your opponent checks in the dark.*

   This behavior _____ the chances of your opponent having a flush draw.

   a. increases

   b. decreases

31. A tight player *calls your flop bet immediately.* This will indicate a _____ hand than if it were a snap-call from a loose player.

   a. weaker

   b. stronger

32. On a flop of 9♦ 8♥ 3♠, you bet and your opponent calls. On a 3♥ turn, you check and *your opponent immediately bets.*

What is the most accurate thing we can say about this quick bet?
   a. It is polarizing: it makes medium-strength hands (like pairs of 9s or 8s) less likely than usual.
   b. It makes medium-strength hands (9s, 8s) more likely than usual.

33. It's heads-up to the turn. You check and your opponent shoves all-in. As you consider, you notice *the pulse in his neck starts to beat very fast.*

What's the most accurate thing we can say about his increased pulse?
   a. It makes it very likely he's bluffing.
   b. It makes it very likely he has a strong hand.
   c. It makes it a bit more likely he's weak, but it's not very reliable.
   d. It makes it a bit more likely he's strong, but it's not very reliable.

34. On the river, *your opponent checks to you while staring at you intently*. He does not usually do this.

   This behavior makes a strong hand...
   a. more likely than usual
   b. less likely than usual

35. Your opponent, before he bets the river, *takes a long time stacking and assembling his chips*. It takes an abnormally long time for him to assemble and place his bet.

   This behavior makes a strong hand...
   a. more likely than usual
   b. less likely than usual

36. On the river, you check, and *your opponent looks over at you several times, studying you in a very obvious way, before betting*.

   This behavior makes a strong hand...
   a. more likely than usual
   b. less likely than usual

37. In a 3-way pot, on the river, the second-to-act player *checks and starts to shuffle his hole cards*.

   This behavior makes a strong hand...
   a. more likely than usual
   b. less likely than usual

38. A player makes a big bet on the river. After he does so, his opponent asks him a question, causing the bettor to *smile in a very broad, dynamic way.*

This behavior makes a strong hand...
   a. more likely than usual
   b. less likely than usual

39. A player bets the river. As he does so, *he makes a subtle palms-face-up gesture with his hand.*

This behavior makes a strong hand...
   a. more likely than usual
   b. less likely than usual
   c. equally as likely as a weak hand

40. On the river, your opponent bets. You can't see his chips clearly and you ask him, "How many chips do you have?" *In response, he lifts his arms so you can see his chips, while making a shrug-like gesture.*

What's the most accurate thing we can say about this behavior?
   a. It makes a strong hand significantly more likely than usual.
   b. It makes a weak hand significantly more likely than usual.
   c. It's ambiguous and can easily be done with both

strong and weak hands.

41. It's heads-up. On the river, your opponent bets, *throwing the chips slightly towards you.*

   This behavior makes a strong hand...
   a. more likely than usual
   b. less likely than usual

42. Which of the following is the most accurate statement about significant bets that are made immediately or near-immediately?

   a. They make medium-strength hands most likely.
   b. They make a polarized hand range likely, while skewing slightly towards stronger hands.
   c. They make a polarized hand range likely, while skewing slightly towards weaker hands.

43. It's heads-up. On the river, your opponent makes a big bet. You notice *he's placed a couple high-denomination chips behind the low-denomination chips*, which makes it hard for you to see the high-denomination chips from where you're sitting.

   This behavior makes a strong hand...
   a. more likely than usual
   b. less likely than usual

44. While post-bet eye contact tells can vary a lot, the most common pattern is for bluffers to _____ than they do when betting strong hands.

   a. make less eye contact

   b. make more eye contact

45. Which of the following eye-contact behaviors is most associated with a bettor who has a strong hand and is relaxed?

   a. A player bets, then stares directly at his opponent without looking away.

   b. A player bets, then avoids eye contact entirely.

   c. A player bets, then makes intermittent, back-and-forth eye contact with his opponent.

46. It's heads-up on the river. *Your opponent says, "All-in" very quietly.* After a pause, he slides in a single stack, *leaving several of his stacks behind.*

This behavior makes a strong hand...

   a. more likely than usual

   b. less likely than usual

47. In a tournament, your opponent shoves on the river a*nd then stands up.* This behavior makes a strong hand…

    a. more likely than usual

    b. less likely than usual

48. Bluffers generally act _____ when an opponent attempts to interact with them.

    a. aggressive or angry

    b. conciliatory or friendly

49. Your opponent shoves on the river. After you think for a few seconds, *he says, "I'm just happy you didn't snap call."*

    What hand range is most likely with this statement?

    a. Bluffs

    b. Strong but not super-strong hands

    c. Very strong hands

50. It's heads-up. On the river, your opponent bets. You start to assemble chips for a call. As you do this, *your opponent lifts up his cards and stares at them for a couple seconds.*

    This behavior makes a strong hand…

    a. more likely than usual

b. less likely than usual

51. Which kind of behavior is more likely to be done purposefully, as a reverse tell?

 a. Subtle

 b. Exaggerated

52. The absence of a tell _____ _____.

 a. usually will indicate the opposite of what the tell indicates

 b. is not necessarily a tell

53. Getting a read indicating a strong hand pre-flop is generally difficult. When you are able to get a strong-hand read pre-flop, it will primarily indicate _____.

 a. TT+ and AT+

 b. TT-AA

 c. AA, KK, and maybe QQ

54. Which phrase best completes this sentence? Getting a read pre-flop is difficult mainly because _____.

 a. many players feel overly confident with AK

 b. most players feel ambivalent about the strength of most hands

 c. light three-bets are so common in most games

today

55. Which phrase best completes this sentence?
    Early in a hand, players with very strong hands,
    whether bettors or non-aggressors, generally avoid
    _____.

    a. taking a long time to act

    b. looking thoughtful

    c. ostentatious behavior

56. Most during-hand talking comes from these
    two types of players: 1) non-aggressors (i.e.,
    checkers and callers) with weak hands, and 2)
    _____.

    a. players who've made big bets with strong hands

    b. players who've made big bets with weak hands
       and bluffs

57. An immediate bet from a player who is first to act
    is _____ to contain information than an
    immediate bet from a second-to-act player.

    a. less likely

    b. more likely

QUIZ ANSWERS

The quiz answers are below, with the number of the question followed by the correct answer. I've included references to the sections where you can find more info.

Again, the online test is at ReadingPokerTells.com/quiz if you want to take it there.

1-b. A player who limps in and acts ostentatiously makes a strong hand less likely than usual. See Hand #2 for more info.

2-b. A player who looks initially at his hole cards for a longer-than-normal time will be less likely than usual to have a strong hand. See Hand #22 for more info.

3-b. Verbal calls make strong hands less likely than usual. See Hand #7 for more info.

4-b. A player who reaches for chips before it's their turn to act and who then bets or raises is less likely than usual to have a strong hand. See Hand #21 for more info.

5-b. A player who is waiting for an opponent to act and who acts confrontationally is less likely than usual to have a strong hand. See Hand #1 for more info.

6-b. An immediate pre-flop raise makes the strongest hands (mainly AA and KK) less likely. See Hand #17 for more info.

7-a. For non-aggressors and waiting-to-act players, weak-hand tells are more common than strong-hand tells. See the River Tells introduction for more info.

8-b. For players making significant bets, it's more common to find strong-hand tells than weak-hand tells. See the *River Tells* introduction for more info.

9-a. A short-stacked player who waits an unusually long time before shoving is more likely than usual to have a strong hand. See Hand #23 for more info.

10-b. Talking and laughing from a pre-flop raiser will make a strong hand less likely than usual. See Hand #25 for more info.

11-d. Quick calls of pre-flop three-bets and four-bets will generally be hands around TT-QQ. See Hand #28 for more info.

12-b. Ostentatious behavior on scary boards make strong hands less likely than usual. See Hand #66 for more info.

13-b. A player who double-checks their hole cards and then checks is less likely than usual to have a strong hand. See Hand #35 for more info.

14-a. A player who double-checks their hole cards and then bets is more likely to have a strong hand. See Hand #78 for more info.

15-b. Talking when checking makes a strong hand less likely than usual. See Hand #36 for more info.

16-b. Verbal exclamations that happen immediately after board cards arrive make it less likely than usual that a player has a strong hand. See Hand #40 for more info.

17-d. When an aggressive player calls the flop immediately, it makes many strong hands and draws less likely.

See Hand #44 for more info.

18-a. A passive player's snap-call of a flop bet includes more draws than a snap-call from an aggressive player. See Hand #44 for more info.

19-a. When an opponent takes an abnormally long time to check the flop, it indicates some interest and makes it more likely he will call or raise your bet. See Hand #32 for more info.

20-b. When a player who was previously the aggressor breaks out of his formerly stoic pose, it makes a strong hand less likely than usual. See Hand #48 for more info.

21-a. In general, when the pre-flop raiser immediately checks back, it will make a strong hand more likely. See Hand #50 for more info.

22-a. A casual call of a significant bet, when there is another player with action remaining after the call, makes a strong hand more likely than usual. See Hand #61 for more info.

23-b. When a player ostentatiously looks at an opponent's chips, and then checks, it makes a strong hand less likely than usual. See Hand #63 for more info.

24-b. On a scary flop, an immediate bet makes a very strong hand less likely than usual. See Hand #75 for more info.

25-c. When someone calls for a card, it will usually not be super-honest but it will usually contain some indirect truth. See Hand #33 for more info.

26-a. When a bettor acts confused, it will make a strong hand more likely than usual. See Hand #87 for more info.

27-a. When a bettor flips a chip end-over-end, it indicates relaxation and makes a strong hand more likely than usual. See Hand #91 for more info.

28-a. Leg-shaking from a player making a significant bet will make a strong hand more likely than usual. See Hand #92 for more info.

29-a. Verbal weak-hand statements make strong hands more likely than usual. See Hand #79 for more info.

30-b. A post-flop check-in-the-dark makes a flush draw less likely. See Hand #71 for more info.

31-b. A tight player's snap-call range is stronger than a loose player's snap-call range. See Hand #97 for more info.

32-a. Immediate post-flop bets are polarizing; they make medium-strength hands less likely than usual. See Hand #72 for more info.

33-c. An increase in a player's pulse associated with a significant bet makes a bluff more likely, but it's not a very reliable tell in general. See Hand #74 for more info.

34-b. Checking and staring at an opponent makes defensiveness and a weak hand more likely than usual. See Hand #58 for more info.

35-a. When associated with a bet, hesitations and pauses in gathering chips and betting make a strong hand more likely than usual. See Hand #100 for more info.

36-a. When a player makes an obvious show of studying an opponent before making a significant bet, a strong hand is more likely than usual. See Hand #101 for more info.

37-b. Post-flop, when a player checks and shuffles his cards, this makes a strong hand less likely than usual. See Hand #103 for more info.

38-a. A big, dynamic smile from a player making a significant bet will make a strong hand more likely than usual. See the section *A genuine smile at the 2013 WSOP* (after Hand #104).

39-a. Shrug-like gestures from bettors will make strong hands more likely than usual. See Hand #105 for more info.

40-c. Shrug-like gestures in response to questions about chip-stacks are very ambiguous and hard to get information from. See Hand #106 for more info.

41-a. When a bettor throws chips towards an opponent, however slightly, it makes a strong hand more likely than usual. See Hand #116 for more info.

42-c. Significant bets that are made immediately or near-immediately make a polarized hand range likely, while skewing slightly towards weaker hands. See Hand #72 for more info.

43-a. When a bettor bets in such a way that their bet amount is hard to understand, this makes relaxation and a strong hand more likely than usual. See Hand #124 for more info.

44-a. In general, players who are bluffing make less eye contact than they do when value-betting. See the section *Eye-contact tells from the 2011 WSOP* for more info (after Hand #76).

45-c. Post-bet eye-contact tells can vary a lot and are mostly player-specific. But intermittent, back-and-forth eye-contact from a bettor will make a strong hand significantly more likely. See *Eye-contact tells from the 2011 WSOP* for more info (after Hand #76).

46-a. When a bettor bets in such a way that their bet amount is theoretically hard to interpret, this makes relaxation and a strong hand more likely than usual. See Hand #124 for more info.

47-a. Standing up after a large post-flop bet or all-in is likely to be a sign of relaxation. See Hand #126 for more info.

48-b. Bluffers are generally conciliatory in manner. They generally avoid being perceived as aggressive or angry. See Hand #127 for more info.

49-b. Most statements from a bettor like, "I'm glad you didn't snap-call" will be honest statements representing strong but not super-strong hands. See Hand #130 for more info.

50-b. Opponent behavior that seems to be done in response to an impending call will make strong hands less likely than usual. See Hand #59 for more info.

51-b. Exaggerated behavior is more likely than subtle behavior to be done purposefully, as a reverse/false tell. See Hand #105 for more info.

52-b. The absence of a tell is not necessarily a tell. This was talked about in a few sections in the book. One mention is in the *General Concepts* section of the intro.

53-c. In the rare spots you're able to get a read of strength pre-flop, it will usually indicate QQ+. See *Eye-contact tells from the 2011 WSOP* for more info (after Hand #76).

54-b. Getting a read pre-flop is difficult mainly because most players feel ambivalent about the strength of most hands. See the *Pre-Flop Tells* intro for more info.

55-c. Early in a hand, players with very strong hands, whether bettors or non-aggressors, generally avoid ostentatious behavior. See Hand #25 for more info.

56-a. Most during-hand talking comes from non-aggressors with weak hands and players who've made big bets with strong hands. See the *General Concepts* in the Introduction for more info.

57-b. An immediate bet from a first-to-act player is more likely to contain meaning than an immediate bet from a second-to-act player. See Hand #121 for more info.

POSTSCRIPT: HEALTH ISSUES

This section is not at all poker-related, so feel free to stop reading at any point.

I wanted to include a little about some health issues I've experienced over the past two years, in case any readers have experienced similar things and wanted to talk about them. After I finish this book, I plan on devoting a lot of time to researching my condition and similar ones.

In April of 2015, at the age of 37, I went out for a run and found that I had no energy. It was like a battery had turned off in my body. I went from being in the best shape of my life—exercising 3-4 times a week, quite strong, and very energetic—to being almost energy-less, with significant body and muscle pain. I've been in basically the same state for the past two years, and I've had some cognitive difficulties as well. All of this has dramatically decreased my quality of life.

None of my symptoms have shown up on any medical tests. The group of symptoms, along with normal test results despite them, fit a class of conditions known by many names—Chronic Fatigue Syndrome, Fibromyalgia, Myalgic Encephalomyelitis (ME), Post-Viral Fatigue Syndrome, Central Sensitivity Syndrome (CSS)—but ultimately all it means is that nobody really understands what causes these conditions or how to treat them.

If anyone has any similar experiences, I'd be interested in hearing from you how your condition came about and what you've done to treat it. One of my life goals now is to contribute in some way to learning more about these conditions and how to treat them.

PAT GRELIA
203-268 9542

CPSIA information can be obtained
at www.ICGtesting.com
Printed in the USA
BVHW01s1215291217
503983BV00001B/63/P

9 780984 033355